CRÊPES

Sweet & Savory Recipes for the Home Cook

LOU SEIBERT PAPPAS

Photographs by JEAN-BLAISE HALL

CHRONICLE BOOKS

SAN FRANCISCO

THIS CHRONICLE BOOKS LLC EDITION PUBLISHED IN 2006.

TEXT COPYRIGHT © 1998 BY LOU SEIBERT PAPPAS
PHOTOGRAPHS COPYRIGHT © 1998 BY JEAN-BLAISE HALL

ISBN-10: 0-8118-5681-X
ISBN-13: 978-0-8118-5681-2

THE LIBRARY OF CONGRESS HAS CATALOGED THE PREVIOUS EDITION AS FOLLOWS:
PAPPAS, LOU SEIBERT.
CRÊPES: SWEET AND SAVORY RECIPES FOR THE HOME COOK/BY LOU PAPPAS:
PHOTOGRAPHS BY JEAN-BLAISE HALL.
P.CM.
INCLUDES INDEX.
ISBN 0-8118-1696-6 (PB)
1. PANCAKES, WAFFLES, ETC. I. TITLE.
TX770.P34P36 1998
641.8'15-DC21
97-21346
CIP

MANUFACTURED IN CHINA

DESIGNED BY CAROLE GOODMAN
FOOD AND PROP STYLING BY GEORGE DOLESE
PHOTOGRAPHY ASSISTANT FABRICE POINCELET

6 8 10 9 7

CHRONICLE BOOKS
680 SECOND STREET
SAN FRANCISCO, CA 94107

WWW.CHRONICLEBOOKS.COM

ACKNOWLEDGMENTS

The author would like to thank her dedicated testers and inspirers: Nan Blackledge, Bunny Callahan, Valerie Fife, Tiffany Moore, Naomi Sachs, and Beth Hensperger. Again, a big thank you to a superb editor, Carolyn Miller.

The photographer and stylist would like to thank Conran Shop in Paris for the use of their objects; the Laurens family for the use of their home; Pierre De Gastines and Véronique De Mareuil for the hand-painted porcelain; and the Vergers St. Eustache for a fine selection of fruits and vegetables.

contents

introduction

t h e wonderful wafer-thin French pancakes called crêpes fill a niche in contemporary dining. Made with light sauces and fillings, they suit today's passion for healthy fare.

The word *crêpe* refers both to the individual pancake and the filled creation. Fast to assemble and ballooning with a voluptuous variety of savory fillings—fresh vegetables and herbs, seafood, poultry, and meat—crêpes can serve as appetizers, first courses, and entrées. Filled with seasonal fruit, soufflés, sauces, sorbets, or ice cream, they become sumptuous desserts.

Turning out a batch of the aromatic butter-browned pancakes is a rewarding endeavor. Assembling them is swift and can often be done ahead. With a stack of these tender discs on hand, you will have myriad serving possibilities for a happy repast any time of day.

Crêpes are ideal to make in advance and refrigerate or freeze, to fill later for a party or informal gathering. They are easy, dramatic, and fun to serve. One option is to stage a kitchen party and let guests spoon on their own fillings.

Crêpes may be made with either plain or sweetened batters. Incorporating different flours into the batter varies the taste. Savory batter can be based on whole-wheat flour or a variety of specialty flours, such as blue cornmeal, buckwheat, garbanzo, or chestnut, all available in bulk in many natural food stores or gourmet markets. Fresh herbs can be used to color and flavor savory crêpes. Sweet crêpes are enhanced by flavorings such as liqueurs, extracts, or fruit zest.

Crêpes star when it comes to versatility. Their fillings can be complex and sophisticated or as simple as a dollop of herb butter, a dice of chilies, or crumbled sheep or goat cheese. Or, for sweet bitefuls, tuck in some grated bittersweet chocolate or white or dark chocolate chips, spread with jam and sprinkle with powdered sugar, or sprinkle with sugar and splash with lemon juice.

Crêpes may be filled and folded in various shapes for a decorative presentation. Ideal to serve around the clock—for morning brunch; an elegant lunch; a midday snack; or a dinner entrée, accompaniment, or sweet finale—crêpes are the good cook's best ally. May these recipes bring pleasure to your table.

s a v o r e d for centuries, crêpes are celebrating a revival today, with *crêperies* opening throughout France, America, and elsewhere in the world.

The word *crêpe* is French for pancake, from the Latin *crispus,* meaning crisp. In France, crêpes were originally called *galettes crêpes,* meaning flat cakes. The French pronunciation of the word is with a short *e,* as in *bed.*

Crêpes originated in Brittany, the northwest region of France, where they rarely had fillings and were used as bread. Until about one hundred years ago, all crêpes were made of buckwheat flour.

Today, crêperies that specialize in serving sweet and savory crêpes are found throughout France. The savory pancakes, served as a main course, are usually made of buckwheat flour and called *galettes,* or *galettes sarrasines,* while dessert crêpes are made with wheat flour.

Until recently, crêpes were cooked on large cast-iron hot plates heated over a wood fire in a fireplace. The hot plates are now gas or electric heated, and the batter is spread with a wooden spreader and flipped with a wooden spatula.

In France, crêpes are traditionally offered on Candlemas and Shrove Tuesday to celebrate renewal, family life, and hope for good fortune and happiness ahead. It is customary to touch the handle of the frying pan and make a wish while the pancake is turned, holding a coin in the hand. In earlier times, in French rural society, farmers offered crêpes to their landowners as a symbol of allegiance.

Crêpes are popular not only throughout France, but elsewhere in Europe, where the pancakes go by other names and adaptations, including Italian *crespelle,* Hungarian *palacsintas,* Jewish *blintzes,* Scandinavian *plattars,* Russian *blini,* and Greek *kreps.*

Making Crêpes

for preparing crêpes, select a 6- or 7-inch French crêpe pan, an omelet pan, or a heavy, preferably nonstick, skillet. A larger size, 9 or 10 inches in diameter, is also useful for some recipes. The smaller size is most often recommended in the recipes here. (The dimensions refer to the interior diameter of the pan.)

Three different tools may be used to mix the batter: a blender, a food processor, or a whisk. My favorite is a blender, because it makes a smooth batter in 5 seconds and is good for pouring. Be careful not to overprocess if you use a food processor, as the batter can become foamy. It can be difficult to achieve a smooth batter when using a whisk.

Prepare the batter at least 1 hour before cooking. For the tenderest crêpes, let the batter sit for 2 hours before cooking. The resting time allows the flour to absorb the liquid and the foam to dissipate. Cover and refrigerate the batter if it is to sit for longer than 1 hour.

Crêpe batter should be about as thick as heavy cream. If it is too thick, thin it with a little water. If it is too thin, additional flour can be added. Different flours have different thickening properties, and moisture in the flour can vary the amount of liquid needed.

Fresh herbs, such as minced garlic chives, dill, tarragon, basil, oregano, and flat-leaf parsley, or liqueurs such as rum, brandy, Calvados, and Cointreau add a delightful flavor to crêpes made for specific fillings.

Premeasure the batter for each crêpe by either using a ladle or a small ¼-cup measure for pouring. Plan to use 2 or 3 tablespoons of batter for the 6- or 7-inch crêpes and about ¼ cup for 9- or 10-inch crêpes. Heat the pan over medium-high heat and, once it is hot, coat it with butter or oil. Lift the pan off the heat as you pour the batter into the pan, and simultaneously tilt the pan in all directions so the batter quickly covers the surface of the pan. If the first crêpe has a hole or two on its surface, quickly add a few more drops of batter to fill them in. After cooking the first crêpe, adjust the heat as necessary. Stir the batter between pourings.

When the crêpe is almost dry on the top and golden brown on the edges (after about 1 minute), it is time to turn it. Use a small spatula to loosen the edge of the crêpe, then turn it over with the spatula or your fingers. Cook the crêpe on the second side, about 15 seconds longer, or until it is lightly browned underneath. Once cooked, invert the crêpe onto a plate or pie pan. Repeat with the remaining batter, stacking the crêpes. If you plan to serve them immediately, cover the pan with aluminum foil and keep them warm in a 200-degree-F oven for a few minutes.

STORING AND REHEATING CRÊPES

i f you do not plan to serve crêpes immediately, stack and package them for later use. Wrap them in plastic wrap and slip them in a self-sealing plastic bag. Crêpes can be refrigerated for up to 3 days or frozen for up to 2 months. It is a good idea to wrap them in the quantities desired for later serving. Thaw frozen crêpes in the refrigerator or at room temperature. (It takes just 15 minutes for a stack of 4 crêpes to thaw.) Bring them to room temperature before separating them. To reheat, wrap them in aluminum foil and reheat in a preheated 325-degree-F oven for 10 to 15 minutes. Once warm, they will separate with ease for filling.

SHAPING CRÊPES

c r ê p e s may be shaped in a variety of styles, depending on the kind of filling and the way you want to present them. Before you fill them, observe which side of the crêpe looks best, and plan to place it facing outward. Generally, the most attractive side is the one that was cooked first (this is known as the face of the crêpe); the other side tends to be lighter in color and spotted. The amount of filling used will vary with each recipe and the way the crêpes are served. Generally, use ¼ to ½ cup of filling for the 6-inch size, and ½ cup or more for the 9-inch size. The following ways to fold crêpes are popular. For baking and presentation, crêpes may be served with their rolled edges placed either up or down.

1| THE ROLL, OR FOLD-OVER: Place a crêpe, face-side down, on a

plate, pan, or work surface, and spoon the filling in a ribbon down the center of the crêpe. Fold over one side, almost covering the filling, then fold over the opposite side, making a neat packet with the filling showing at each end. This style is good for both entrée and dessert crêpes.

2| **THE CIGARETTE:** Place a crêpe, face-side down, on a plate, pan, or work surface, and spoon or spread the filling along one edge. Roll up, forming a small cylinder. This style is good for appetizer crêpes.

3| **THE ENVELOPE:** Place a crêpe, face-side down, on a plate, pan, or work surface, and spoon the filling into the center of it. Fold over both sides, then fold the bottom of the crêpe over about half of the filling. Fold the top of the crêpe down over both sides and turn over. This style encases the filling completely and is traditional for entrée crêpes.

4| **THE BATON:** Place a crêpe, face-side down, on a plate, pan, or work surface and spoon the filling into the center of it. Fold over both sides, then roll up from the bottom of the crêpe, forming a neat, cylindrical shape. This style is good for appetizers and desserts.

5| **THE HALF-MOON:** Place a crêpe, face-side down, on a plate, pan, or work surface. Spread or spoon the filling on half of the crêpe and fold the crêpe in half. This is useful for soufflé fillings.

6| **THE SANDWICH, OR TRIANGLES:** Place a crêpe, face-side down, on a plate, pan, or work surface. Spread the filling entirely over its surface. Cover with a second crêpe, face-side up. Press lightly to seal. Serve whole as a first course or cut into 6 or 8 triangles for appetizers.

9

7| **THE STACK:** Place crêpes, face-side up, on a work surface. Spread the filling over a crêpe, leaving about a ¼-inch border around the edge. Place

4|

5|

6|

second crêpe on top and spead filling over it. Repeat to stack and spread filling over each crêpe. Chill or bake, then cut into wedges to serve as an appetizer, first course, or entrée.

8| **THE TRIANGULAR FOLD:** Place a crêpe, face-side down, on a work surface. Fold it in half, then fold it in half again, forming a triangle 4 layers thick. This is good for crêpes that are flamed in a sauce.

9| **THE SQUARE FOLD:** Place a crêpe, face-side down, on a work surface and spoon the filling into the center. Fold over the 4 sides halfway toward the center, forming a square shape with an open center. This is good for large crêpes and is the typical fold for French buckwheat *galettes*, along with a triangular shape made by folding 3 sides over. Sometimes this folded *galette* is served flipped over.

10| **THE CUP:** Place 6-inch crêpes in greased muffin cups or custard cups, carefully arranging the top in flutes. Fill and bake for entrées.

11| **THE PURSE:** Place a crêpe, face-side down, on a work surface and spoon the filling in the center. Bring up the sides, forming pleats on top, and tie with a chive or green onion top. This fold is appropriate for appetizers.

8|

10|

11|

Problem-Solving

Are there too many bubbles in the batter?
If so, the batter was beaten too long at too high a speed in the blender or food processor. Let it stand longer before baking.

Do your crêpes have a lacy pattern?
The batter may be too thin; mix 1 or 2 tablespoons of flour into the batter.

Are the edges of the crêpes crisp, with a tendency to crack?
The pan is too hot; decrease the heat. Or, the batter may be too thin; whisk or blend 1 to 2 tablespoons flour into the batter.

Do small holes appear in the crêpes?
Use more batter to completely cover the pan.

Does the batter curdle like scrambled eggs?
There is too much butter or oil in the pan.

Does the batter refuse to coat the bottom of the pan with ease?
The batter is too thick; mix 1 to 2 tablespoons milk or water into the batter.

basic crêpes

SAVORY CRÊPES 13

Herb Crêpes

Sun-Dried Tomato Crêpes

Blue Cornmeal Crêpes

Buckwheat Galettes

Corn Flour Crêpes

Cornstarch Crêpes

Garbanzo Flour Crêpes

Chestnut-Garbanzo Flour Crêpes

Whole-Wheat Crêpes

Chestnut Flour Crêpes

DESSERT CRÊPES 16

Espresso Crêpes

Chestnut Flour Dessert Crêpes

Chocolate Crêpes

SAVORY CRÊPES

these versatile, multipurpose crêpes, and the variations that follow, are great for savory fillings. Keep a stack on hand in the freezer for unexpected guests. The crêpes will quickly defrost at room temperature, then separate with ease.

It takes just 2 or 3 teaspoons of butter to coat the pan for a batch of crêpes. A paper butter wrapper with a small amount of butter on it is a fast way to achieve this. For health reasons, if you prefer you may use 2 tablespoons canola, safflower, or olive oil in the savory crêpe batter instead of melted butter, but the flavor will be slightly different. Oil may also be used to coat the pan, but butter is preferable for its browning effect.

2	large eggs
1 CUP	milk
⅓ CUP	water
1 CUP	all-purpose flour, preferably bleached
¼ TEASPOON	salt
2 TABLESPOONS	butter, melted, plus 2 or 3 teaspoons butter for coating the pan

in a blender or food processor, blend the eggs, milk, water, flour, salt, and the 2 tablespoons melted butter for 5 seconds, or until smooth. Stir down and repeat if necessary. Or, to mix by hand, sift the flour into a medium bowl and add the salt. Whisk the eggs until blended, mix in the milk and water, and whisk this mixture into the flour and salt; stir in the 2 tablespoons melted butter. Cover and refrigerate for at least 1 hour (though 2 hours is preferable) or up to 24 hours.

Gently stir the batter if it has separated. Heat a seasoned 6- or 7-inch nonstick crêpe pan over medium-high heat until hot. (Use a 9- or 10-inch pan for larger crêpes.) Coat the pan lightly with butter, lift the pan from the heat, and pour in 2 or 3 tablespoons of batter for a 6- or 7-inch pan, or about ¼ cup for a 9- or 10-inch pan, tilting and rotating the pan to coat the surface. Cook until almost dry on top and lightly browned on the edges, about 1 minute. Loosen the edges with a metal spatula and flip the crêpe over using your fingers or the spatula, then cook the other side for about 15 seconds, or until lightly browned. Turn the crêpe out onto a clean tea towel to cool. Repeat with the remaining batter, wiping the pan with butter as needed and stacking the crêpes as they are cooked.

For serving immediately, cover the crêpes with aluminum foil and keep them warm in a preheated 200-degree-F oven. For serving later, wrap them in plastic wrap in quantities intended for each use and slip them in a self-sealing plastic bag. Refrigerate crêpes for up to 3 days, or freeze them for up to 2 months.

*Makes sixteen to eighteen 6- or 7-inch crêpes,
or ten to twelve 9- or 10-inch crêpes*

HERB CRÊPES: Follow the savory crêpe recipe and add ¼ cup minced fresh chives, basil, or flat-leaf parsley to the batter while blending it. Or, for pale green mixed-herb crêpes, use ½ cup mixed minced fresh chives, green onion tops, flat-leaf parsley, tarragon, marjoram, and basil.

SUN-DRIED TOMATO CRÊPES: Follow the savory crêpe recipe and add ¼ cup minced oil-packed sun-dried tomatoes to the batter while blending it.

BLUE CORNMEAL CRÊPES: Follow the savory crêpe recipe, but replace the 1 cup all-purpose flour with ⅔ cup all-purpose flour and ⅔ cup blue cornmeal.

BUCKWHEAT GALETTES: Follow the savory crêpe recipe, but replace the 1 cup all-purpose flour with ⅔ cup all-purpose flour and ⅔ cup buckwheat flour.

CORN FLOUR CRÊPES: Follow the savory crêpe recipe, but replace the 1 cup all-purpose flour with ⅔ cup all-purpose flour and ⅔ cup corn flour (which is more finely ground than cornmeal).

CORNSTARCH CRÊPES: Follow the savory crêpe recipe, but replace the 1 cup all-purpose flour with 1 cup cornstarch and add ⅛ teaspoon baking soda.

GARBANZO FLOUR CRÊPES: Follow the savory crêpe recipe, but replace the 1 cup all-purpose flour with ⅔ cup all-purpose flour and ⅔ cup garbanzo flour.

CHESTNUT-GARBANZO FLOUR CRÊPES: Follow the savory crêpe recipe, but replace the 1 cup all-purpose flour with ⅔ cup garbanzo flour and ½ cup chestnut flour.

WHOLE-WHEAT CRÊPES: Follow the savory crêpe recipe, but replace the 1 cup all-purpose flour with 1 cup whole-wheat flour or 1 cup whole-wheat pastry flour, or ½ cup all-purpose flour and ½ cup whole-wheat flour.

CHESTNUT FLOUR CRÊPES: Follow the savory crêpe recipe, but replace the 1 cup all-purpose flour with ⅔ cup all-purpose flour and ½ cup chestnut flour.

DESSERT CRÊPES

YOU can vary the flavoring of these sweet crêpes to suit the intended filling: rum with chocolate or nuts, Cointreau with orange or lemon, amaretto with almonds, Frangelico with hazelnuts, framboise with raspberries or strawberries, Cognac or brandy with stone fruits such as peaches or nectarines, and Calvados with apples.

2	large eggs
1 CUP	milk
⅓ CUP	water
1 CUP	all-purpose flour, preferably bleached
2 TABLESPOONS	sugar
1 TEASPOON	vanilla extract
1 TABLESPOON	rum, Cointreau, amaretto, brandy, or other liqueur (optional)
2 TABLESPOONS	butter, melted, plus 2 to 3 teaspoons for coating the pan

IN a blender or food processor, blend the eggs, milk, water, flour, sugar, vanilla, optional flavoring, and the 2 tablespoons melted butter for 5 seconds, or until smooth. Stir down and repeat, if necessary. Or, to mix by hand, sift the flour into a medium bowl and add the sugar. Whisk the eggs until blended, mix in the milk, water, vanilla, and optional flavoring, and whisk this mixture into the flour; stir in the 2 tablespoons melted butter. Cover and refrigerate for at least 1 hour (2 hours is preferable) or up to 24 hours.

Gently stir the batter if it has separated. Heat a seasoned 6- or 7-inch nonstick crêpe pan over medium-high heat until hot. (Use a 9- or 10-inch pan for larger crêpes.) Wipe the pan lightly with butter, lift the pan from the heat, and pour in 2 to 3 tablespoons of batter for a 6- or 7-inch pan, or about ¼ cup for a 9- or 10-inch pan, tilting and rotating the pan to coat the surface. Cook until almost dry on top and lightly browned on the edges, about 1 minute. Loosen the edges with a metal spatula and flip the crêpe over using your fingers or the spatula, then cook the other side for about 15 seconds, or until lightly browned. Turn the crêpe out onto a clean tea towel to cool. Repeat with the remaining batter, wiping the pan with butter as needed and stacking the crêpes as they are cooked.

For serving immediately, cover the crêpes with aluminum foil and keep them warm in a preheated 200-degree-F oven. For serving later, wrap them in plastic wrap in quantities intended for each use and slip them into a self-sealing plastic bag. Refrigerate the crêpes for up to 3 days, or freeze them for up to 2 months.

Makes sixteen to eighteen 6- or 7-inch crêpes,
or ten to twelve 9- or 10-inch crêpes.

ESPRESSO CRÊPES: Grind 2 tablespoons coffee beans to a fine powder and add to the dessert crêpe batter when blending it.

CHESTNUT FLOUR DESSERT CRÊPES: Follow the dessert crêpe recipe, but replace the 1 cup all-purpose flour with ⅔ cup all-purpose flour and ½ cup chestnut flour.

CHOCOLATE CRÊPES: Follow the dessert crêpe recipe, but replace the 1 cup all-purpose flour with ¾ cup all-purpose flour and ⅓ cup unsweetened cocoa. Replace the 2 tablespoons sugar with ¼ cup sifted powdered sugar.

appetizer crêpes

APPLE & BRIE HALF-MOON CRÊPES 19

APRICOT-PISTACHIO GOAT CHEESE TRIANGLES 20
Cherry-Hazelnut Goat Cheese Triangles

PESTO & CHEESE TRIANGLES 21
Sun-Dried Tomato & Cheese Triangles

BEGGAR'S PURSES WITH CAVIAR 23

*BUCKWHEAT GALETTES WITH
SMOKED SALMON AND RED ONIONS* 25
Herb Crêpe Batons with Smoked Trout

*CHESTNUT-GARBANZO FLOUR CRÊPES
WITH BASIL AND CHIVES* 26

HUMMUS PINWHEELS 27

RICOTTA PILLOWS 29

PARTY CRÊPE STACK WITH PESTO FILLINGS 31

*WHOLE-WHEAT CRÊPES WITH
SUN-DRIED TOMATOES AND ARUGULA* 33

APPLE & BRIE HALF-MOON CRÊPES

pick flavor-packed apples, such as Fujis, Braeburns, or Granny Smiths, to complement the Brie in these attractive packets. Serve as a first course or as an accompaniment to a lunch salad.

EIGHT 6- OR 7-INCH	garbanzo flour or savory crêpes (see page 13)
¾ CUP (6 OUNCES)	firm ripe Brie, thinly sliced
2	small Fuji, Braeburn, or Granny Smith apples or Anjou or Bosc pears, quartered, cored, and thinly sliced
1 TABLESPOON	butter, melted
¼ CUP	walnuts or pecans, chopped

prepare the crêpes. Preheat the oven to 375 degrees F. Place a crêpe in a 12-by-18-inch baking pan and arrange a slice of the cheese and 3 slices of apples evenly over half of it; fold over. Repeat with the remaining crêpes. Brush the crêpes with butter and sprinkle with nuts. Bake in the oven for 8 to 10 minutes, or until the cheese is melted. Serve at once.

Makes 8 first course or side-dish servings

19

APRICOT-PISTACHIO GOAT CHEESE TRIANGLES

tangy-sweet apricots and roasted pistachios enliven the goat cheese spread in these sophisticated appetizers. For an attractive party tray, offer two or three kinds of triangles with wine.

SIX 6- OR 7-INCH	garbanzo flour or savory crêpes (see page 13)
¾ CUP (6 OUNCES)	ricotta cheese
½ CUP (4 OUNCES)	fresh white goat cheese or light cream cheese at room temperature
2 TEASPOONS	brandy or Cognac
½ CUP	dried apricots, finely chopped, plus 2 dried apricots cut into strips for garnish
⅓ CUP	pistachios

prepare the crêpes. In a bowl, mash together the ricotta, goat cheese or cream cheese, and brandy or Cognac and mix in the chopped apricots and pistachios. Spread one-third of the filling in a thin layer over each of 3 crêpes. Cover each with a second crêpe, face-side up. Press down lightly to seal.

Cover each "sandwich" with plastic wrap and refrigerate until ready to serve, or up to 1 day in advance. Cut each "sandwich" into 8 wedges, forming triangles. Garnish with a thin strip of apricot.

Makes 24 appetizers

CHERRY-HAZELNUT GOAT CHEESE TRIANGLES: Omit the apricots and pistachios, and substitute ½ cup dried tart cherries, chopped, and ⅓ cup skinned toasted hazelnuts, chopped (see page 46). Instead of brandy or Cognac, flavor with kirsch, if you wish. Garnish each appetizer with a dried cherry.

PESTO & CHEESE TRIANGLES

sandwich crêpes with a zestful pesto and cheese filling, then cut them into triangles for make-ahead appetizers.

SIX 6- OR 7-INCH	garbanzo flour, herb, or savory crêpes (see page 13)
¾ CUP (6 OUNCES)	ricotta cheese
½ CUP (4 OUNCES)	fresh white goat cheese at room temperature
⅓ CUP	minced fresh basil
¼ CUP	pine nuts, toasted (see Note)
3	shallots or green onions, finely chopped
2	garlic cloves, minced
¼ CUP	grated Parmesan cheese
	Fresh basil leaves for garnish

prepare the crêpes. In a small bowl, mash together the ricotta and goat cheeses and mix in the basil, pine nuts, shallots or onions, garlic, and Parmesan. Spread one-third of the filling in a thin layer over each of 3 crêpes. Cover each with another crêpe, face-side up. Press down lightly to seal.

Cover each pair of filled crêpes with plastic wrap and refrigerate until ready to serve, or up to 1 day in advance. Cut each sandwich into 8 wedges, forming triangles. Garnish each with a basil leaf.

Makes 24 appetizers

NOTE: To toast pine nuts, place the nuts in a pie pan and heat in a preheated 325-degree-F oven for 6 to 8 minutes, or until lightly browned.

SUN-DRIED TOMATO & CHEESE TRIANGLES: Prepare the Pesto and Cheese Triangles, reducing the basil to 2 tablespoons and adding ⅓ cup chopped oil-packed sun-dried tomatoes with herbs. Garnish each triangle with a leaf of parsley or a ⅛-inch slice of green onion top.

BEGGAR'S PURSES WITH CAVIAR

these neat little crêpe packets, tied with a chive, hold a biteful of golden caviar. They are lovely with champagne.

SIXTEEN 6- OR 7-INCH	savory or herb crêpes, or buckwheat galettes (see page 13)
1 CUP	light sour cream or plain yogurt
3 OUNCES (⅓ CUP)	golden, black, or red caviar
1 TABLESPOON	minced fresh chives
16	chives, about 6 inches long, or green onion tops

prepare the crêpes or galettes. Cover them with aluminum foil and keep them warm in a 200-degree-F oven, or cover and reheat them in a baking pan in a preheated 325-degree-F oven for 5 to 10 minutes, or until heated through.

Working quickly, assemble the purses by spooning a tablespoonful of sour cream or yogurt and a teaspoonful of caviar onto the center of each crêpe; sprinkle with minced chives. Gather each crêpe into a bundle the shape of a drawstring purse and tie with a chive or onion top. Serve immediately.

Makes 16 appetizers

BUCKWHEAT GALETTES WITH SMOKED SALMON AND RED ONIONS

for a festive occasion such as New Year's Eve, a wedding reception, or an anniversary party, this appetizer is an ideal choice. It also makes a savory first course or light entrée for company. The galettes may be made in advance, then assembled and refrigerated. Bring almost to room temperature before serving.

TWELVE 6- OR 7-INCH	buckwheat galettes (see page 13)
½ CUP (4 OUNCES)	fresh white goat cheese or natural cream cheese at room temperature
1 CUP (8 OUNCES)	ricotta cheese
¾ CUP	minced shallots or red onion
1½ TEASPOONS	minced fresh dill, or ½ teaspoon dried dill
2 TABLESPOONS	minced fresh chives
6 OUNCES	thinly sliced smoked salmon, cut into strips
	Whole chives or chive blossoms for garnish

prepare the crêpes. In a bowl, combine the cheeses, shallots or onion, dill, and chives. Spread 6 of the crêpes with a thin layer of the cheese mixture and cover with salmon strips. Top each with another crêpe. Garnish with chives or chive blossoms. Serve whole as a first course or entrée, or cut into wedges as an appetizer.

Makes 6 first-course servings or 36 appetizers

HERB CRÊPE BATONS WITH SMOKED TROUT: In place of buckwheat galettes, use 12 herb crêpes (see page 14) and fill them with 1½ cups (12 ounces) room-temperature natural cream cheese mixed with 6 ounces smoked trout, chopped. Fold each into a baton (see page 9) and cut each one on the diagonal to make bite-sized morsels.

CHESTNUT-GARBANZO FLOUR CRÊPES WITH BASIL AND CHIVES

al giusto has owned Giusto Vita-Grain Flour Mills in South San Francisco for over half a century. The charming silver-haired miller remembers his mother mixing a handful of chestnut flour into the garbanzo *crespelle* batter. After the thin pancakes were cooked, they were drizzled with olive oil and rolled up for eating out-of-hand. A few leaves of basil, oregano, and garlic chives or goat cheese are delicious stuffed inside.

EIGHT 6- OR 7-INCH   chestnut-garbanzo flour crêpes (see page 13)
Extra-virgin olive oil for drizzling
Fresh basil leaves or oregano leaves
Fresh garlic chives

prepare the crêpes. Cover them with aluminum foil and keep them warm in a 200-degree-F oven, or cover and reheat them in a baking pan in a preheated 325-degree-F oven for 5 to 10 minutes, or until heated through. Drizzle each crêpe with olive oil, add a few leaves of basil or oregano and 2 or 3 garlic chives, and roll up. Serve at once as an appetizer or as an accompaniment to a meal.

Makes 8 rolls

CHESTNUT-GARBANZO FLOUR CRÊPES WITH CHEESE, BASIL, AND CHIVES: Crumble Bulgarian or Greek feta cheese or fresh white goat cheese over the warm crêpes, add the herbs, and roll up.

26

HUMMUS PINWHEELS

the garbanzo bean and sesame paste spread called hummus creates a creamy, garlic-spiced filling for crêpes.

FOUR 9- OR 10-INCH	garbanzo flour or savory crêpes (see page 13)
	HUMMUS
ONE	15-ounce can garbanzo beans
3 TABLESPOONS	fresh lemon juice
2	garlic cloves, chopped
3 TABLESPOONS	chopped fresh flat-leaf parsley
2 TABLESPOONS	chopped green onion tops or chives
¼ TEASPOON	salt
½ TEASPOON	ground cumin
	Freshly ground pepper
1 TO 2 TABLESPOONS	plain sesame oil
8 OUNCES	alfalfa sprouts
	Chopped pistachio nuts for garnish

prepare the crêpes. *TO MAKE THE HUMMUS:* Rinse the garbanzo beans in a strainer under cold running water; drain. In a blender or food processor, combine the beans with the lemon juice, garlic, parsley, green onion, salt, cumin, pepper to taste, and sesame oil, and process until almost smooth.

TO ASSEMBLE THE CRÊPES: Lay out a crêpe on a work surface, face-side down. Spread the crêpe with a ⅜-inch layer of hummus, sprinkle with sprouts, and roll up. Repeat to fill all the crêpes. Cover with plastic wrap and refrigerate. When ready to serve, cut into ¾-inch slices. Arrange on a plate, cut-side up, and garnish with chopped nuts.

Makes 4 dozen appetizers

RICOTTA PILLOWS

this classic Italian dish is known as *bocconcini di Parma*. Each ricotta-filled crêpe ring makes a sumptuous appetizer to savor with a glass of Merlot. Or, serve 4 per person as an entrée.

EIGHT 6- OR 7-INCH	garbanzo flour, chestnut-garbanzo flour, or savory crêpes (see page 13)
2 CUPS (16 OUNCES)	ricotta cheese
2 TABLESPOONS	butter at room temperature
2	shallots, minced
2	eggs
¾ CUP (3 OUNCES)	grated Parmesan cheese
	Salt and ground white pepper
⅛ TEASPOON	freshly grated nutmeg

prepare the crêpes. Drain the ricotta cheese for about 45 minutes in a colander lined with a double thickness of cheesecloth.

In a small skillet over medium-low heat, melt 1 teaspoon of the butter and sauté the shallots until golden. In a medium bowl, beat the eggs lightly and mix in the ricotta, Parmesan cheese, remaining butter, shallots, salt and pepper to taste, and nutmeg. Spoon about 3 tablespoons of filling in a ribbon down the center of each crêpe and roll to enclose. Cover with plastic wrap and refrigerate for at least 30 minutes.

Place each chilled roll on a board and cut it into 4 pieces. Arrange the cut crêpes in a buttered 9-by-13-inch baking dish, standing cut-side down and touching. If desired, make ahead to this point, cover with plastic wrap, and refrigerate for several hours. To bake, preheat the oven to 375 degrees F. Bake in the oven for 15 minutes, or until heated through. Serve at once.

Makes 32 appetizers or 8 entrée servings

PARTY CRÊPE STACK WITH PESTO FILLINGS

sun-dried tomato and pesto cheeses alternate as fillings for stacked crêpes. When cut into wedges, they make handsome appetizers. For a shortcut version, purchase sun-dried tomato and basil pestos from a gourmet shop. Serve the wedges on small appetizer plates for a neat presentation.

SIX 6- OR 7-INCH	savory or garbanzo flour crêpes (see page 13)

SUN-DRIED TOMATO FILLING

¾ CUP (6 OUNCES)	fresh white goat, ricotta, or Mascarpone cheese at room temperature
2 TABLESPOONS	milk
½ CUP	oil-packed sun-dried tomatoes, chopped
¼ CUP	minced fresh flat-leaf parsley
2 TABLESPOONS	minced fresh basil
2	garlic cloves, minced
3 TABLESPOONS	pine nuts, toasted (see page 21)

BASIL PESTO FILLING

2 CUPS	packed fresh basil leaves
3 TABLESPOONS	pine nuts, toasted (see page 21)
2	garlic cloves, crushed
¼ CUP	extra-virgin olive oil
3 TABLESPOONS	grated Parmesan cheese
⅓ CUP (3 OUNCES)	ricotta cheese
⅓ CUP (3 OUNCES)	light cream cheese at room temperature

6	oil-packed sun-dried tomato halves, diced, for garnish

prepare the crêpes. *TO MAKE THE SUN-DRIED TOMATO FILLING:* In a bowl, mix the cheese and milk together until blended. Stir in the sun-dried tomatoes, parsley, basil, garlic, and pine nuts.

TO MAKE THE BASIL PESTO FILLING: In a blender or food processor, whirl the basil, pine nuts, and garlic until minced. Blend in the oil, add the Parmesan, ricotta, and cream cheeses, and process until blended.

Lay out 1 crêpe and spread with one-third of the sun-dried tomato filling; cover with another crêpe and spread with one-third of the basil pesto filling. Repeat, alternating the fillings and layering the crêpes. Decorate the top with the diced tomatoes. Cover and refrigerate for at least 1 hour. Cut into wedges and serve on small plates. To serve as finger food, omit the top cheese layer.

Makes 12 appetizer wedges

WHOLE-WHEAT CRÊPES WITH SUN-DRIED TOMATOES AND ARUGULA

sweet dried tomatoes, peppery arugula, and creamy cheese make flavorful first-course crêpe sandwiches or triangular appetizers.

TWELVE 6- OR 7-INCH	whole-wheat crêpes or buckwheat galettes (see page 13)
¾ CUP (6 OUNCES)	light cream cheese at room temperature
½ CUP (4 OUNCES)	ricotta cheese
4	shallots or green onions (include part of the green tops), finely chopped
3 TABLESPOONS	chopped arugula
2 DOZEN	oil-packed sun-dried tomato halves, drained and chopped
2 TABLESPOONS	melted butter or olive oil
	Arugula leaves or nasturtium blossoms for garnish

prepare the crêpes. Preheat the oven to 400 degrees F. In a medium bowl, combine the cheeses, shallots or green onions, and arugula. To assemble, place 3 of the crêpes on a greased baking sheet; spread each with one-third of the cheese mixture and cover with one-third of the tomatoes. Top each with another crêpe and drizzle with the butter or oil.

Bake in the oven for 5 to 6 minutes, or until just heated through. Serve whole as a first course, garnished with arugula or nasturtiums, or cut each into 6 wedges and pass as an appetizer.

Makes 6 first-course servings or
3 dozen appetizers

vegetable side-dish crêpes

BLUE CORN CRÊPES WITH LEEKS & MUSHROOMS 35

ASPARAGUS & HAM CRÊPES 37

ARTICHOKE CRÊPES, MONTEREY STYLE 38

ROASTED GARLIC, TOMATO & PESTO CRÊPES 41

POTATO, ONION & SAGE CRÊPES 43

SALAD BASKET CRÊPES WITH GRAPES,
BLUE CHEESE & HAZELNUTS 45

SPINACH & RICOTTA CRÊPES 47

TOMATO CRÊPES WITH RATATOUILLE 49

SUMMER SQUASH & RED ONION CRÊPES 51

GINGERED GREEN LENTIL CRÊPES 52

WILD MUSHROOM CRÊPES 55

CARROT & ZUCCHINI CRÊPES 57

BROCCOLI, RED ONION &
PRESERVED LEMON CRÊPES 58

BLUE CORN CRÊPES WITH LEEKS & MUSHROOMS

caramelized leeks and woodsy mushrooms fill these crunchy blue corn crêpes. Serve them with roast chicken and a salad of Comice pears, toasted hazelnuts, and blue cheese on greens.

EIGHT 6- OR 7-INCH	blue corn or whole-wheat crêpes (see page 13)
3 TABLESPOONS	extra-virgin olive oil
1¼ POUNDS	leeks, finely chopped (white part only)
½ CUP (4 OUNCES)	cultivated white mushrooms, sliced
1	egg
¾ CUP (6 OUNCES)	ricotta cheese or plain yogurt
½ CUP (2 OUNCES)	shredded Gruyère or Jarlsberg cheese
2	garlic cloves, minced
3 TABLESPOONS	minced fresh chives or green onion tops
2 TEASPOONS	minced fresh tarragon, or ½ teaspoon dried tarragon
	Salt

prepare the crêpes. Preheat the oven to 350 degrees F. In a large skillet over medium heat, heat 1 tablespoon of the oil and sauté the leeks until they are soft and caramelized, about 15 minutes. Turn them out of the pan. Add 1 tablespoon of the oil to the pan and sauté the mushrooms over medium heat for 1 minute; add to the leeks. In a large bowl, combine the egg, ricotta or yogurt, Gruyère, garlic, chives or green onions, tarragon, salt, leeks, and mushrooms, mixing lightly.

Spoon ½ cup of the filling onto the center of each crêpe and fold it like an envelope. Arrange in a greased 9-by-13-inch baking dish. Brush the tops of the crêpes with the remaining 1 tablespoon oil. Bake in the oven for 10 to 15 minutes, or until heated through.

Makes 8 crêpes; serves 4

ASPARAGUS & HAM CRÊPES

fresh asparagus heralds springtime and makes a delectable entrée or first course encased in crêpes. Omit the ham for a vegetarian dish or to serve as a vegetable accompaniment to grilled salmon, skewered jumbo shrimp, or baked trout. These crêpes may be assembled in advance and refrigerated for last-minute baking.

EIGHT 6- OR 7-INCH	garbanzo flour or savory crêpes (see page 13)
1	large sweet white or red onion, chopped
1½ POUNDS	asparagus spears, cut into 1-inch diagonal lengths
1	egg
¾ CUP (6 OUNCES)	ricotta cheese or natural cream cheese at room temperature
½ CUP (2 OUNCES)	shredded Gruyère or Emmenthal cheese
3 TABLESPOONS	grated Parmesan cheese
2	garlic cloves, minced
2 TABLESPOONS	minced fresh flat-leaf parsley
2 TEASPOONS	minced fresh tarragon or dill, or ½ teaspoon dried tarragon or dill
2 OUNCES	honey-baked ham or Black Forest ham, julienned

prepare the crêpes. Preheat the oven to 350 degrees F. Steam the onion and asparagus in a covered container over boiling water until the asparagus is crisp-tender, about 5 to 7 minutes. In a medium bowl, beat the egg and mix in the cheeses, garlic, parsley, tarragon or dill, ham, and steamed vegetables.

Spoon ½ cup of the filling in a ribbon down the center of each crêpe and roll to enclose. Arrange in a greased 9-by-13-inch baking dish. Bake in the oven for 10 to 15 minutes, or until heated through. Serve at once.

Makes 8 crêpes; serves 4

ARTICHOKE CRÊPES, MONTEREY STYLE

castroville, a rural coastal town on the California Monterey Peninsula, is famous for its artichokes. Each plant produces mature artichokes in several sizes. The largest one crowns the top of the fernlike plant, and the tiny 1- to 2-inch artichokes are scattered below. This recipe is a great way to savor the "baby" artichokes. When well trimmed and cooked to tenderness, the entire vegetable is edible.

EIGHT 6-INCH	garbanzo flour, herb, or savory crêpes (see page 13)
12 OUNCES	1-inch baby artichokes, or one 10-ounce package frozen artichoke hearts, thawed and diced
2 TABLESPOONS	fresh lemon juice for water bath (optional)
1	egg
½ CUP (4 OUNCES)	ricotta cheese
½ CUP (4 OUNCES)	light cream cheese at room temperature
2	garlic cloves, minced
2	shallots or green onions (include part of the green tops), finely chopped
1 TABLESPOON	minced fresh basil
2 OUNCES	diced ham or smoked trout
½ CUP (2 OUNCES)	shredded Jarlsberg or Gruyère cheese
	Fresh basil leaves for garnish

38

prepare the crêpes. Preheat the oven to 350 degrees F. If using fresh artichokes, remove all but the pale inner leaves. Halve the artichokes and immediately drop them into a bowl of water mixed with the lemon juice as you prepare them (this prevents them from darkening). Drain the artichokes and cook them in a small amount of boiling salted water until tender, about 15 to 20 minutes. Drain, let cool, and dice the artichokes.

In a medium bowl, whisk the egg and stir in the ricotta, cream cheese, garlic, shallots or green onions, basil, artichokes, ham or trout, and shredded cheese. Spoon ½ cup of the filling into the center of each crêpe, folding it like an envelope to enclose the filling. Arrange in a greased 9-by-13-inch baking dish. Bake in the oven for 10 to 15 minutes, or until heated through. Garnish with basil leaves and serve immediately.

Makes 8 crêpes; serves 4

ROASTED GARLIC, TOMATO & PESTO CRÊPES

ON a balmy summer evening, serve these crêpes at room temperature; heat them to serve on a cool night. It is a good idea to roast the garlic and tomatoes in advance, ready for last-minute assembly of the crêpes. You might complete the menu with a Caesar salad and finish off with orange or mango sorbet.

EIGHT 6- OR 7-INCH	garbanzo flour, corn, or savory crêpes (see page 13)
6	Roma tomatoes, cut into ½-inch dice
1	head garlic
1 TABLESPOON	olive oil
	Salt and freshly ground pepper
1 CUP	fresh basil leaves, minced
¼ CUP	minced fresh flat-leaf parsley
3	green onions (include the green tops), finely chopped
3 TABLESPOONS	pine nuts or pistachios, chopped
1 CUP (8 OUNCES)	ricotta cheese
½ CUP (2 OUNCES)	shredded Monterey Jack, Jarlsberg, or Emmenthal cheese
2 TABLESPOONS	grated Parmesan cheese

41

prepare the crêpes. Preheat the oven to 375 degrees F. Place the tomatoes and garlic in a baking dish and drizzle with oil, then wrap the garlic in aluminum foil. Bake in the oven for 30 to 35 minutes, or until the garlic is soft; let cool. Continue to roast the tomatoes for 20 to 30 minutes longer, or until slightly dry; season with salt and pepper and let cool.

Squeeze the garlic into a medium bowl. Mix in the basil, parsley, green onions, nuts, and cheeses. Gently stir in the tomatoes.

The crêpes may be served at room temperature or baked. To bake, reduce the oven temperature to 350 degrees F. Spoon ½ cup of filling down the center of each crêpe and roll. Place in a greased 9-by-13-inch baking pan. Bake in the oven for 10 to 15 minutes.

Makes 8 crêpes; serves 4

POTATO, ONION & SAGE CRÊPES

the duo of red-skinned new potatoes and sweet onions makes an appealing vegetarian-style entrée or first course. Or let it accompany grilled skirt steak or butterflied leg of lamb.

EIGHT 6- OR 7-INCH	herb, garbanzo flour, or savory crêpes (see page 13)
1½ POUNDS	small new potatoes, such as Red Bliss or Yukon Gold
3 TABLESPOONS	dry white wine
1 TABLESPOON	extra-virgin olive oil
2	sweet white or red onions, chopped
1	egg
¾ CUP (6 OUNCES)	ricotta cheese
⅓ CUP (3 OUNCES)	light cream cheese at room temperature
½ CUP (2 OUNCES)	shredded Gruyère or Emmenthal cheese
2	garlic cloves, minced
3 TABLESPOONS	minced fresh chives, plus extra for garnish
2 TEASPOONS	minced fresh sage, or ½ teaspoon dried sage

prepare the crêpes. Preheat the oven to 350 degrees F. Steam the potatoes over boiling water in a covered container until tender, about 10 to 15 minutes. Slice the potatoes, sprinkle with the wine, and let cool. Meanwhile, in a medium skillet over medium heat, heat the oil and sauté the onions until soft, about 10 minutes.

In a large bowl, combine the egg, cheeses, garlic, chives, sage, potatoes, and onions, mixing lightly. Spoon ½ cup of filling in a ribbon down the center of each crêpe and roll to enclose. Arrange in a greased 9-by-13-inch baking dish. Bake in the oven for 10 to 15 minutes, or until heated through. Garnish with chives.

Makes 8 crêpes; serves 4

SALAD BASKET CRÊPES WITH GRAPES, BLUE CHEESE & HAZELNUTS

at a waterfront *crêperie* in Toulouse, France, waitresses set forth plate-sized crêpes shaped like a basket and filled with mesclun embellished with Roquefort cheese and toasted hazelnuts. Under the shade of the red-and-white-striped canopy, this dish was casual summertime dining at its best.

FOUR 9- OR 10-INCH	buckwheat galettes, or herb or garbanzo flour crêpes (see page 13)
	SHALLOT VINAIGRETTE
3 TABLESPOONS	extra-virgin olive oil
1½ TABLESPOONS	red wine vinegar
1 TEASPOON	Dijon mustard
1	shallot, minced
	Salt and freshly ground pepper
4 HANDFULS	mixed baby greens
¼ CUP (2 OUNCES)	Gorgonzola, Roquefort, or blue cheese
1 CUP	seedless red or green grapes, or 1 Comice or Anjou pear, cored and thinly sliced
¼ CUP	hazelnuts, toasted, skinned, and coarsely chopped (see Note)

prepare the crêpes. Cover the crêpes with aluminum foil and keep warm in a preheated 300-degree-F oven, or cover and reheat them in a baking pan in a preheated 325-degree-F oven for 5 to 10 minutes.

TO MAKE THE VINAIGRETTE: In a jar or small bowl, shake or whisk together the olive oil, vinegar, mustard, shallot, and salt and pepper to taste until blended.

Place the salad greens in a large bowl. Toss the greens with the vinaigrette. Place a crêpe on a dinner plate, spoon the greens into the center, and fold up the sides to encase the greens and form a basket shape. Scatter the cheese, fruit, and nuts over the greens. Repeat to fill all the crêpes.

Makes 4 crêpes; serves 4

NOTE: To toast and skin hazelnuts, preheat the oven to 325 degrees F. Place the nuts in a pie pan and bake for 8 minutes, or until lightly toasted. Wrap the hazelnuts in a cloth towel and rub to remove most of the skins. Let cool before using.

Spinach & Ricotta Crêpes

spinach-plumped crêpes complement fish or poultry; try them with grilled salmon, swordfish kabobs, or roast or sautéed chicken. Another time, use red Swiss chard instead of spinach in this recipe.

EIGHT 6- OR 7-INCH	savory, garbanzo flour, or herb crêpes (see page 13)
2 POUNDS	fresh spinach (about 2 bunches), stemmed and washed
1¼ CUPS (10 OUNCES)	ricotta cheese
1	egg, beaten
½ CUP (2 OUNCES)	shredded Jarlsberg cheese or crumbled feta or aged goat cheese
¼ TEASPOON	freshly grated nutmeg
	Salt and freshly ground pepper
1 TABLESPOON	olive oil or melted butter
2 TABLESPOONS	grated Parmesan cheese

prepare the crêpes. Preheat the oven to 350 degrees F. Cook the spinach in a covered pan over medium heat for 1 minute, or until slightly limp. Drain the spinach and press out the excess water with the back of a large spoon, then chop finely. In a medium bowl, mix together the ricotta, egg, Jarlsberg, feta, or goat cheese, nutmeg, spinach, and salt and pepper to taste.

Spoon ½ cup of filling in a ribbon down the center of each crêpe and roll up. Arrange in a greased 9-by-13-inch baking pan. Brush the tops with the olive oil or butter and sprinkle with the Parmesan cheese. Bake in the oven for 10 to 15 minutes, or until heated through. Serve at once.

Makes 8 crêpes; serves 4

TOMATO CRÊPES WITH RATATOUILLE

nestled in the spectacular wine country of South Africa, the elegant Grand Roche Hotel in Paarl serves crêpes in many styles, including these, flavored with sun-dried tomatoes, nuggeted with walnuts, and flecked with fresh dill or basil. The classic eggplant, zucchini, and pepper mélange is a favorite filling.

EIGHT 6- OR 7-INCH	sun-dried tomato crêpes (see page 13)
2 TABLESPOONS	olive oil
3	shallots, minced
½	eggplant, diced (8 ounces)
4	baby zucchini, diced
1	red bell pepper, roasted, peeled, and diced (see Note)
1	green bell pepper, roasted, peeled, and diced
3	Roma tomatoes, chopped
2	garlic cloves, minced
3 TABLESPOONS	mixed minced fresh basil and flat-leaf parsley
½ CUP	tomato juice
	Salt and freshly ground pepper
¾ CUP (3 OUNCES)	shredded Gruyère cheese

GARNISH

Crème fraîche or plain yogurt

Fresh basil leaves

prepare the crêpes. Preheat the oven to 350 degrees F. In a large skillet over medium heat, heat 1 tablespoon of the oil and sauté the shallots, eggplant, zucchini, peppers, and tomatoes for 5 to 7 minutes. Add the garlic, basil and parsley, tomato juice, and salt and pepper to taste. Cover and simmer until the vegetables are soft, about 10 to 12 minutes. Let cool slightly and mix in the cheese.

Spoon ½ cup of the filling in a ribbon down the center of each crêpe and roll to enclose. Arrange in a greased 9-by-13-inch baking dish. Brush with the remaining 1 tablespoon oil. Bake in the oven for 10 to 15 minutes, or until heated through. Garnish with crème fraîche or yogurt and basil leaves. Serve at once.

Makes 8 crêpes; serves 4

NOTE: To roast and peel peppers, hold the peppers over an open flame or put under a preheated broiler and turn frequently until completely charred on all sides. Put the peppers in a loosely closed paper bag until cool, about 15 minutes. Remove the peppers from the bag and rub off the blackened skin with your fingers.

SUMMER SQUASH & RED ONION CRÊPES

the abundant summer harvest finds a savory niche in these roasted garlic and tomato-laced crêpes.

EIGHT 6- OR 7-INCH	garbanzo flour or savory crêpes (see page 13)
1¼ POUNDS	mixed baby yellow summer squash, pattypans, and zucchini
	Salt
1 TABLESPOON	olive oil
1	large red onion, finely chopped
¼ CUP	minced fresh flat-leaf parsley, plus fresh flat-leaf parsley sprigs for garnish
ONE	8-ounce can tomato sauce
3 TABLESPOONS	roasted garlic tomato paste
2 TEASPOONS	minced fresh oregano, or ½ teaspoon dried oregano
	Freshly ground pepper
¾ CUP (3 OUNCES)	shredded sharp white Cheddar cheese

prepare the crêpes. Preheat the oven to 350 degrees F. Slice the squash, pattypans, and zucchini thinly and sprinkle with salt. Let stand for 15 minutes, then rinse thoroughly under cold water and pat dry. In a large skillet over medium heat, heat the oil and sauté the onion for 3 minutes, or until soft. Add the minced parsley, tomato sauce, and tomato paste and simmer for 5 minutes, uncovered, to reduce slightly. Add the squash, pattypans, and zucchini and cook for 2 to 3 minutes, or until crisp-tender. Mix in the oregano, salt and pepper to taste, and cheese. Let cool slightly.

Spoon about ½ cup filling in a ribbon down the center of each crêpe and roll to enclose. Arrange in a greased 9-by-13-inch baking dish. Bake in the oven for 10 to 15 minutes. Garnish with parsley leaves and serve at once.

Makes 8 crêpes; serves 4

GINGERED GREEN LENTIL CRÊPES

ginger-spiked green. lentils create a marvelous filling for tender crêpes. These wholesome rolls are great for a potluck gathering or a party meal. On other occasions, serve the lentils hot as a winter stew or cool as a summer salad drizzled with a balsamic vinaigrette, with the rolled warm crêpes on the side in a basket.

SIXTEEN 6- OR 7-INCH	garbanzo flour, blue cornmeal, or whole-wheat crêpes (see page 13)
1 POUND	green lentils
1	large sweet onion, chopped
2	carrots, peeled and chopped
4 CUPS	water
2	garlic cloves, minced
2 TEASPOONS	minced fresh thyme, or ½ teaspoon dried thyme
	Salt and freshly ground pepper
2 TABLESPOONS	red wine vinegar
2 TABLESPOONS	balsamic vinegar
ONE	6-ounce can tomato paste
6	sun-dried tomato halves, finely chopped
¼ CUP	mixed minced fresh chives, flat-leaf parsley, and oregano
1 TABLESPOON	minced fresh ginger
1½ CUPS (6 OUNCES)	shredded Jarlsberg, Monterey Jack, or Cheddar cheese
2 TABLESPOONS	extra-virgin olive oil
¼ CUP	grated Parmesan cheese

prepare the crêpes.

TO MAKE THE FILLING: In a large saucepan, combine the lentils, onion, carrots, water, garlic, thyme, and salt and pepper to taste. Bring to a boil, cover, and simmer for 25 to 30 minutes, or until the lentils are almost tender but still have a slight crunch. Add the vinegars, tomato paste, dried tomatoes, herbs, and ginger, and heat through. (The filling may be made in advance and reheated.)

Preheat the oven to 350 degrees F. Spoon ½ cup of filling in a ribbon down the center of each crêpe, sprinkle with shredded cheese, and roll to enclose. Arrange in two greased 9-by-13-inch baking dishes. Brush the tops of the crêpes with the oil and sprinkle with Parmesan cheese. Bake in the oven for 10 to 15 minutes, or until heated through. Serve at once.

Makes 16 crêpes; serves 8

WILD MUSHROOM CRÊPES

select a mixture of domestic and wild mushrooms for these woodsy crêpes. They make a delicious partner to venison steaks, leg of lamb, grilled salmon or albacore, or duck breast, or they can be served on their own for a vegetarian feast.

EIGHT 6- TO 7-INCH	buckwheat galettes or blue cornmeal or savory crêpes (see page 13)
3 TABLESPOONS	extra-virgin olive oil, or 2 tablespoons porcini oil and 1 tablespoon olive oil
3	shallots or green onions (include half the green onion tops), chopped
1 POUND	mixed mushrooms: cultivated whites, shiitakes, oysters, portobellos, and morels, or 14 ounces cultivated white mushrooms and 1 ounce assorted dried mushrooms, soaked in warm water to cover for 15 minutes
1	egg
¾ CUP (6 OUNCES)	ricotta cheese or fresh white goat cheese or light cream cheese at room temperature
½ CUP (2 OUNCES)	shredded Gruyère or Jarlsberg cheese
2	garlic cloves, minced
2 TEASPOONS	minced fresh tarragon, or ½ teaspoon dried tarragon
	Salt and freshly ground pepper
2 TABLESPOONS	grated Parmesan cheese

prepare the crêpes. Preheat the oven to 350 degrees F. In a large skillet over medium-high heat, heat 2 tablespoons of the olive oil and sauté the shallots or onions for 1 to 2 minutes. Add the mushrooms and quickly heat through, about 1 minute. Transfer mushrooms to a bowl and let cool.

   In a medium bowl, whisk the egg and mix in the ricotta, goat, or cream cheese, Gruyère cheese, garlic, tarragon, salt and pepper to taste, and sautéed vegetables. Spoon ½ cup of filling in a ribbon down the center of each crêpe, and roll up to enclose. Arrange in a greased 9-by-13-inch baking dish, brush with the remaining 1 tablespoon oil, and sprinkle with the Parmesan cheese. Bake in the oven for 10 to 15 minutes, or until heated through. Serve at once.

Makes 8 crêpes; serves 4

CARROT & ZUCCHINI CRÊPES

shredded bundles of vegetables fill corn crêpes for an appealing side dish. To serve as an entrée, pair these with Roasted Garlic, Tomato & Pesto Crêpes (page 41) or Chicken, Sweet Corn & Red Pepper Crêpes (page 77).

EIGHT 6- OR 7-INCH	corn flour, blue cornmeal, or savory crêpes (see page 13)
1 TABLESPOON	olive oil
4	carrots, peeled and shredded
4	zucchini, shredded
3	green onions (include half of the green tops), chopped
2	eggs
¾ CUP (6 OUNCES)	ricotta cheese or light cream cheese at room temperature
¾ CUP (3 OUNCES)	shredded Gruyère, Emmenthal, or Jarlsberg cheese
¼ CUP	minced fresh flat-leaf parsley, plus parsley leaves for garnish
2	garlic cloves, minced
¼ TEASPOON	ground cumin
⅛ TEASPOON	freshly grated nutmeg
	Salt and freshly ground pepper
¼ CUP	pistachios, chopped

prepare the crêpes. Preheat the oven to 350 degrees F. In a large skillet over medium heat, heat the oil and sauté the carrots, zucchini, and onion for 2 to 3 minutes, or until the vegetables are soft. In a medium bowl, beat the eggs and mix in the cheeses, parsley, garlic, cumin, nutmeg, salt and pepper to taste, nuts, and vegetables.

Spoon ½ cup of filling in a ribbon down the center of each crêpe and roll. Arrange in a greased 9-by-13-inch baking dish. Bake in the oven for 10 to 15 minutes. Garnish with parsley leaves.

Makes 8 crêpes; serves 4

BROCCOLI, RED ONION &
PRESERVED LEMON CRÊPES

preserved lemon adds a salty tang to broccoli florets in this healthful dish. This is especially good with seafood: sautéed scallops or shrimp, grilled swordfish, or mahimahi.

A Moroccan condiment, preserved lemons are available in specialty markets, yet it is easy to cure your own with the recipe included here. Use them in a salsa for grilled fish or black beans, or as a condiment for brown rice, roasted peppers, or eggplant.

EIGHT 6- OR 7-INCH	savory, garbanzo flour, or whole-wheat crêpes (see page 13)
2 POUNDS	broccoli
4 TEASPOONS	olive oil
1	large sweet white or red onion, chopped
¾ CUP	plain yogurt
⅓ CUP (1½ OUNCES)	shredded Jarlsberg, Gruyère, or Emmenthal cheese
2	garlic cloves, minced
2 TABLESPOONS	minced fresh flat-leaf parsley, plus parsley leaves for garnish
2 TABLESPOONS	minced preserved lemon (recipe follows), or 2 teaspoons grated lemon zest

prepare the crêpes. Preheat the oven to 350 degrees F. Cut the broccoli into florets (reserve the stems for another use). Steam the broccoli florets in a covered container over boiling water until crisp-tender, about 7 minutes.

In a small skillet, heat 1 teaspoon of the oil over medium heat and sauté the onion for 5 minutes, or until soft. In a medium bowl, combine the yogurt, cheese, garlic, parsley, preserved lemon or lemon zest, steamed broccoli, and sautéed onion.

Lay out a crêpe face-side down. Spoon ½ cup of the filling in a ribbon on the center of each crêpe, and roll to enclose. Arrange in a greased 9-by-13-inch baking dish. Brush the tops of the crêpes with the remaining 3 teaspoons oil. Bake in the oven for 10 to 15 minutes, or until heated through. Garnish with parsley leaves and serve at once.

Makes 8 crêpes; serves 4

PRESERVED LEMONS

8	lemons, preferably Meyer, washed
½ CUP	coarse sea salt
2	cinnamon sticks
4	bay leaves
	Fresh lemon juice, if needed

cut each lemon into quarters from the top, cutting almost but not quite through the peel. Sprinkle the pulp with a little salt and pack into a large sterilized jar. Add the cinnamon, bay leaves, and the remaining salt and press down. The juice from the lemons should cover the fruit. If not, add more lemon juice to cover. Cover with a lid. Let sit at room temperature in a dark place for 3 weeks, turning the jar over occasionally.

Store in the refrigerator for up to 6 months. To use, scrape off and discard the inside pulp, then rinse the preserved peel thoroughly and prepare as needed. Preserved lemon is also good minced or julienned and used with vegetables, beans, rice, or fish.

entrée crêpes

BREAKFAST CRÊPES

fill-your-own breakfast crêpes are a congenial treat for houseguests or for special breakfasts like Christmas or New Year's. Serve a stack of warm crêpes with an array of fillings: whipped honey, raspberry sauce or another berry syrup, cinnamon sugar, and bowls of berries and plain yogurt. Sliced mangoes heated in maple syrup are another option.

SIXTEEN 6- OR 7-INCH	savory or dessert crêpes (see pages 13 and 16)
1 CUP	raspberry sauce (see page 88) or commercial berry syrup
2½ CUPS	fresh strawberries, raspberries, or blueberries
½ CUP	whipped honey
1 CUP	plain yogurt
1 TABLESPOON	ground cinnamon
¼ CUP	sugar
1	mango, peeled, cut from the pit, and diced
½ CUP	maple syrup

prepare the crêpes. Cover them with aluminum foil and keep warm in a 200-degree-F oven, or cover and reheat them in a baking pan in a preheated 325-degree-F oven for 5 to 10 minutes, or until heated through.

Pour the raspberry sauce into a small pitcher. Spoon the berries, whipped honey, and yogurt into separate bowls. Combine the cinnamon and sugar in a small bowl to make cinnamon sugar. Heat the mango in the maple syrup until heated through and spoon into a bowl. Set out the fillings and let guests fill their own crêpes.

Makes 16 crêpes; serves 8

BAKED EGG CRÊPE CUPS

crêpes tucked into muffin cups make easy fluted pastry cases for baked eggs and mushrooms. It takes just a few minutes to assemble this eye-catching brunch dish if the crêpes are already made.

FOUR 6- OR 7-INCH	savory crêpes, buckwheat galettes, or garbanzo flour crêpes (see page 13)
	Olive oil for brushing
½ CUP (4 OUNCES)	sliced cultivated white mushrooms
1 TEASPOON	minced fresh tarragon, or ¼ teaspoon dried tarragon
3	shallots or green onions (include the green tops), finely chopped
4	eggs
	Salt and freshly ground pepper
¼ CUP	half-and-half
¼ CUP	shredded Gruyère or Jarlsberg cheese

prepare the crêpes. Preheat the oven to 325 degrees F. Brush 4 muffin pans or custard cups with oil and line each with a cooked crêpe by placing it in the cup, pressing lightly against the bottom, and pleating the crêpe edges on the sides of the cup.

In a small bowl, mix the mushrooms, tarragon, and shallots or green onions together. Spoon one-quarter of this mixture into each crêpe. Break 1 egg into each crêpe, sprinkle with salt and pepper, and spoon 1 tablespoon half-and-half over each. Top each crêpe cup with 1 tablespoon cheese.

Bake in the oven for 16 to 18 minutes, or until the yolks are set but still runny inside. Let cool for 2 to 3 minutes, then remove from the pans and serve at once.

Makes 4 crêpes; serves 4

CHEESE BLINTZES

blintzes are a classic Sunday brunch delicacy topped with sour cream and tart cherry preserves. Cornstarch creates a particularly tender crêpe.

TWELVE 6- OR 7-INCH	cornstarch crêpes (see page 13)
1½ CUPS (12 OUNCES)	farmer's cheese, ricotta cheese, or lowfat cottage cheese, puréed
½ CUP (4 OUNCES)	light cream cheese at room temperature
2	egg yolks
1 TABLESPOON	packed brown sugar
1 TEASPOON	vanilla extract
2 TABLESPOONS	unsalted butter, melted

GARNISH
Sour cream
Tart cherry preserves or fresh strawberries or blueberries

prepare the crêpes. Preheat the oven to 375 degrees F. In a food processor or a medium bowl, mix together the cheeses, egg yolks, sugar, and vanilla until blended. Place a rounded tablespoon of filling in the center of each crêpe and fold in the sides to make an envelope shape.

Place the envelopes seam-side down in a buttered 12-by-18-inch baking pan. Brush with butter. Bake in the oven for 10 to 12 minutes, or until heated through. Garnish each blintz with a spoonful of sour cream and preserves or berries. Serve at once.

Makes 12 blintzes; serves 6

CHESTNUT FLOUR CRÊPES WITH FIGS & GOAT CHEESE

luscious, juicy figs or nectarines mingle with goat cheese and hazelnuts for a delightful autumn treat. Serve as an entrée for brunch or lunch, or as a dessert for a dinner menu—perhaps fettuccine with pesto and grilled lemon chicken breasts.

EIGHT 6- OR 7-INCH	chestnut flour or dessert crêpes (see pages 13 and 16)
1 CUP (8 OUNCES)	soft white goat cheese at room temperature
2 TABLESPOONS	half-and-half
1 TABLESPOON	Cointreau or brandy
6	fresh figs, stemmed and sliced, or 4 nectarines, peeled, pitted, and sliced
3 TABLESPOONS	hazelnuts, toasted, skinned, and chopped (see Note, page 46)
2 TABLESPOONS	raw sugar

prepare the crêpes. Cover them with aluminum foil and keep them warm in a 200-degree-F oven, or cover and reheat them in a baking pan in a preheated 325-degree-F oven for 5 to 10 minutes, or until heated through.

In a medium bowl, combine the cheese with the half-and-half and the liqueur or brandy until blended. Spoon 2 tablespoons of the mixture down the center of each crêpe. Top each with one-eighth of the fruit and roll up. Divide the filled crêpes among 4 warm plates. Sprinkle the crêpes with the nuts and sugar. Serve at once.

Makes 8 crêpes; serves 4

BRETON CRÊPES WITH POACHED EGGS & MUSHROOMS

breton *crêperies* have popularized this combination for lunch or supper: a mélange of sautéed shallots, mushrooms, and tomatoes on a buckwheat galette, topped with a poached egg.

FOUR 9- OR 10-INCH	buckwheat galettes or savory crêpes (see page 13)
1 TABLESPOON	extra-virgin olive oil
3	shallots or green onions (white part only), finely chopped
1	garlic clove, minced
½ CUP (4 OUNCES)	sliced cultivated white mushrooms
1	Roma tomato, diced
2 TABLESPOONS	minced fresh flat-leaf parsley
4	eggs
	Salt and freshly ground pepper

prepare the crêpes. Cover them with aluminum foil and keep warm in a 200-degree-F oven, or cover and reheat them in a baking pan in a preheated 325-degree-F oven for 5 to 10 minutes, or until heated through. In a large skillet over medium heat, heat the oil and sauté the shallots or green onions and garlic for 1 to 2 minutes. Add the mushrooms and sauté for 1 to 2 minutes, or until soft; stir in the tomatoes and parsley.

Meanwhile, poach the eggs in barely simmering water just until the whites are set and the yolks are still runny; drain. Lay out each crêpe on a warm plate. Spoon one-quarter of the filling into the center of each crêpe and top with an egg. Season with salt and pepper. Fold over 3 sides to form a triangular shape. Serve at once.

Makes 4 crêpes; serves 4

FOUR-CHEESE ROLLS WITH CHERRY TOMATOES

four cheeses meld in an ethereal filling for rolled crêpes. Cherry tomatoes and basil strike a colorful accent. Serve these with snow peas and a salad adorned with grapes or nasturtium blossoms.

Eight 6- or 7-inch	buckwheat galettes or herb crêpes (see page 13)
	FOUR-CHEESE FILLING
1¼ CUPS (10 OUNCES)	ricotta cheese
¾ CUP (6 OUNCES)	fresh white goat cheese at room temperature
½ CUP (2 OUNCES)	shredded Gruyère or Jarlsberg cheese
2 TABLESPOONS	grated Parmesan cheese
1	egg
⅛ TEASPOON	freshly grated nutmeg
1 TABLESPOON	olive oil
2 TABLESPOONS	grated Parmesan cheese
½ CUP	red cherry tomatoes, halved
½ CUP	gold cherry tomatoes
¼ CUP	fresh basil leaves, sliced

prepare the crêpes. Preheat the oven to 375 degrees F.
TO MAKE THE FILLING: In a medium bowl, mix the ricotta cheese, goat cheese, Gruyère, Parmesan, egg, and nutmeg.

Spoon one-eighth of the filling down the center of each crêpe and make an envelope fold. Arrange in a greased 9-by-13-inch baking dish. Brush the tops of the crêpes with the olive oil and sprinkle with the Parmesan cheese. Bake in the oven for 10 to 12 minutes. Garnish with tomatoes and sprinkle with basil. Serve at once.

Makes 8 crêpes; serves 4

TURKEY-MUSHROOM CRÊPE CAKE

this handsome multilayered crêpe stack is a fine way to utilize the leftover turkey from a roasted bird. A light Mornay sauce binds the sautéed mushrooms and turkey.

EIGHT 6- OR 7-INCH	savory or garbanzo flour crêpes (see page 13)
	MORNAY SAUCE
2 TABLESPOONS	butter
4 TABLESPOONS	flour
1½ CUPS	milk
¾ CUP	chicken broth
	Salt and freshly ground pepper
¼ TEASPOON	freshly grated nutmeg
1 CUP (4 OUNCES)	shredded Gruyère cheese
2 TABLESPOONS	butter
2	shallots or green onions (white part only), chopped
1½ CUPS (12 OUNCES)	sliced cultivated white mushrooms
4½ CUPS (1¼ POUNDS)	diced cooked turkey or chicken
3 TABLESPOONS	minced fresh flat-leaf parsley
¼ CUP	shredded Gruyère cheese

prepare the crêpes.

TO MAKE THE MORNAY SAUCE: In a medium saucepan over medium heat, melt the butter, add the flour, and cook, stirring, until the mixture is bubbly, about 1 minute. Add the milk, broth, salt and pepper to taste, and nutmeg and whisk until the sauce thickens and comes to a boil. Reduce the heat and simmer, whisking occasionally, for 2 to 3 minutes. Stir in the Gruyère. Remove the pan from the heat and set aside.

In a large skillet over medium heat, melt 2 tablespoons butter and sauté the shallots for 1 minute, or until translucent. Add the mushrooms and sauté for 2 minutes, or until soft. Reserve ⅓ cup of the Mornay sauce for topping. Mix the mushrooms, turkey, and parsley into the pan with the remaining sauce.

Place a crêpe in a greased 9-inch pie pan and cover it with ⅔ cup of the filling. Cover with a second crêpe and repeat filling, stacking, and layering the remaining crêpes. Leave the top crêpe unfilled; spread the reserved Mornay sauce over it and sprinkle with the remaining ¼ cup Gruyère. If desired, cover and refrigerate for up to 24 hours. Allow refrigerated crêpe cake to come to room temperature before baking.

To bake, preheat the oven to 375 degrees F. Bake for 20 to 25 minutes, or until heated through. Cut into wedges and serve at once.

Makes 8 crêpes; serves 6

CANNELLONI

Make these sumptuous Italian crêpes in advance and refrigerate for up to 24 hours.

SIXTEEN 6- OR 7-INCH	garbanzo flour or savory crêpes (see page 13)
3 TABLESPOONS	extra-virgin olive oil
1	large onion, chopped
2	garlic cloves, minced
1	pound ground turkey
1	pound ground veal
1 CUP (8 OUNCES)	ricotta cheese
¾ CUP (3 OUNCES)	grated Parmesan cheese
2 CUPS (8 OUNCES)	shredded Monterey Jack or sliced teleme cheese
2	eggs
	Salt and freshly ground pepper
1 TABLESPOON	minced fresh sage, or ¾ teaspoon dried sage
1 TABLESPOON	minced fresh basil
¼ TEASPOON	freshly grated nutmeg

prepare the crêpes. In a large skillet over medium heat, heat 1 tablespoon of the oil and sauté the onion until soft, about 5 minutes. Add the garlic and meats and cook until the meats lose their pink color; let cool slightly. Mix in the ricotta, ½ cup of the Parmesan, the shredded cheese, eggs, salt and pepper to taste, herbs, and nutmeg.

Spoon the filling in a ribbon down the center of each crêpe and roll up to encase. Arrange in a greased 10-by-15-inch baking pan. Brush the tops with the remaining 2 tablespoons olive oil and sprinkle with the remaining Parmesan cheese. Cover and refrigerate for up to 24 hours if making ahead.

To bake, preheat the oven to 350 degrees F. Bake for 15 to 20 minutes. Serve at once.

Makes 16 crêpes; serves 8

SAUSAGE & MUSHROOM CRÊPES

lowfat gourmet sausages, dried cranberries, and portobello mushrooms create soul-satisfying crêpes for company. Assemble these a few hours in advance to avoid last-minute hassle.

EIGHT 6- OR 7-INCH	savory or garbanzo flour crêpes (see page 13)
10 OUNCES	fresh chicken-apple, Italian turkey, or other gourmet sausage
2 TABLESPOONS	extra-virgin olive oil or porcini oil
3	shallots or green onions (white part only), finely chopped
¾ CUP (6 OUNCES)	chopped portobello, shiitake, or cultivated white mushrooms
1	egg or 2 egg whites, slightly beaten
¾ CUP (6 OUNCES)	ricotta cheese or fresh white goat cheese at room temperature
½ CUP (2 OUNCES)	shredded Gruyère or Jarlsberg cheese
2	garlic cloves, minced
2 TEASPOONS	minced fresh tarragon, or ½ teaspoon dried tarragon
⅓ CUP	dried cranberries
2 TABLESPOONS	grated Parmesan cheese

prepare the crêpes. In a saucepan, cover the sausages with water and poach in barely simmering water for 10 minutes, or until cooked through. Let cool, and then skin the sausages and chop coarsely. In a medium skillet over medium heat, heat 1 tablespoon of the oil and sauté the shallots or green onions for 1 or 2 minutes. Add the mushrooms and sauté until just heated through, about 1 minute; turn out of the pan to cool.

In a medium bowl, combine the egg or egg whites, ricotta or goat cheese, shredded cheese, garlic, tarragon, sausage, cranberries, and sautéed mushrooms and shallots.

Spoon ½ cup of the filling in a ribbon down the center of each crêpe and roll up. Arrange in a greased 9-by-13-inch baking dish, brush with the remaining 1 tablespoon oil, and sprinkle with the Parmesan cheese. Cover and refrigerate for up to 24 hours if making ahead. Allow refrigerated crêpes to come to room temperature before baking.

To bake, preheat the oven to 350 degrees F. Bake in the oven for 10 to 15 minutes, or until heated through. Serve at once.

Makes 8 crêpes; serves 4

CHICKEN, SWEET CORN &
RED PEPPER CRÊPES

choose these flavor-filled crêpes for a harvest treat. Good accompaniments include coleslaw, tiny green beans, and fresh peaches with vanilla bean ice cream or frozen yogurt.

EIGHT 6- OR 7-INCH	savory crêpes (see page 13)
½	onion
	Salt
ONE	½-inch piece fresh ginger
3	boneless, skinless chicken breast halves
2	ears fresh white or yellow corn
2 TABLESPOONS	extra-virgin olive oil
½ CUP	diced red bell pepper
1	shallot or green onion (include half the green tops), chopped
1	egg
¾ CUP (6 OUNCES)	ricotta cheese
½ CUP (2 OUNCES)	shredded Jarlsberg or Monterey Jack cheese
2	garlic cloves, minced
2 TEASPOONS	minced fresh sage, or ½ teaspoon dried sage
	Salt and freshly ground pepper
¾ CUP (3 OUNCES)	grated Parmesan cheese

prepare the crêpes. Place ½ inch water in a large skillet. Add the onion, salt, and ginger and bring just to a simmer over low heat. Add the chicken and poach until just opaque throughout, about 10 to 15 minutes. Remove from the liquid, let cool, and dice.

Cut the corn kernels from the cobs. In a large skillet over medium heat, heat 1 tablespoon of the oil and sauté the corn, peppers, and shallot or green onion for 2 to 3 minutes, or until the vegetables are soft. In a medium bowl, whisk the egg and mix in the ricotta, shredded cheese, garlic, sage, salt and pepper to taste, chicken, and vegetables.

Preheat the oven to 350 degrees F. Spoon ½ cup of filling onto the center of each crêpe and fold like an envelope to enclose the filling. Arrange the crêpes in a greased 9-by-13-inch baking dish, brush them with the remaining 1 tablespoon oil, and sprinkle with the Parmesan cheese. Bake in the oven for 10 to 15 minutes, or until heated through. Serve at once.

Makes 8 crêpes; serves 4

BUCKWHEAT GALETTES WITH HAM & GRUYÈRE

ti couz, a charming Breton *crêperie* in San Francisco, specializes in buckwheat galettes folded into neat square packets with the rounded sides tucked underneath, a favorite here in San Francisco and a classic in France.

FOUR 9- OR 10-INCH	buckwheat galettes or savory crêpes (see page 13)
4	thin ham slices
1 CUP (4 OUNCES)	shredded Gruyère, Jarlsberg, or Emmenthal cheese
1 TABLESPOON	melted butter or olive oil
2 TABLESPOONS	grated Parmesan cheese

prepare the crêpes. Preheat the oven to 350 degrees F. Cover each crêpe with a slice of ham and ¼ cup of the shredded cheese. Fold over 4 sides to encase the filling and make a square packet. Place each packet upside-down on a greased baking sheet. Brush with the melted butter or oil and sprinkle with the Parmesan cheese. Bake in the oven for 10 to 15 minutes, or until heated through. Serve at once.

Makes 4 crêpes; serves 4

FENNEL & SCALLOP CRÊPES

the licorice tang of fennel complements scallops in this light entrée. A fresh seasonal green vegetable—asparagus, broccoli, Italian green beans, or sugar snap peas—makes a pretty plateful served alongside.

EIGHT 6- TO 7-INCH	garbanzo flour or herb crêpes, buckwheat galettes, or savory crêpes (see page 13)
1	small fennel bulb
2 TABLESPOONS	olive oil
1	shallot or green onion (white part only), finely chopped
12 OUNCES	bay scallops
2 TEASPOONS	minced fresh ginger
⅓ CUP	dry white wine
2 TABLESPOONS	fresh lemon juice
1	egg
¾ CUP (6 OUNCES)	ricotta cheese or light cream cheese at room temperature
2 TEASPOONS	minced fresh tarragon, or ½ teaspoon dried tarragon
	Salt and ground white pepper
½ CUP (2 OUNCES)	shredded Jarlsberg, Gruyère, or Monterey Jack cheese
2 TABLESPOONS	grated Parmesan cheese

prepare the crêpes. Preheat the oven to 350 degrees F. Peel and dice the fennel bulb and chop 2 tablespoons of the feathery fronds. In a large skillet, heat 1 tablespoon of the oil over medium heat and sauté the fennel and shallot or green onion for 1 to 2 minutes, or until crisp-tender. Add the scallops and ginger and sauté 2 minutes, turning the scallops to brown both sides. Pour in the wine and lemon juice, increase the heat to medium-high, and cook until the liquid is reduced to a glaze.

In a medium bowl, whisk the egg and mix in the ricotta or cream cheese, tarragon, salt and pepper to taste, shredded cheese, and scallop mixture. Spoon ½ cup of the filling in a ribbon down the center of each crêpe and roll up. Arrange in a greased 9-by-13-inch baking dish, brush with the remaining 1 tablespoon oil, and sprinkle with the Parmesan cheese. Bake in the oven for 10 to 15 minutes, or until heated through. Serve at once.

Makes 8 crêpes; serves 4

LANGOUSTINE, AVOCADO & MANGO CRÊPES

AN elegant, rich filling of langoustines, avocado, and mango plumps tender crêpes for a rainbow of flavors. These are a sumptuous treat served alfresco for luncheon on a warm summer day. For a first course, a cold cucumber soup topped with yogurt and chives is delightful. A strawberry or raspberry sorbet is nice for a finale.

EIGHT 6- OR 7-INCH	savory or garbanzo flour crêpes (see page 13)
1 TABLESPOON	olive oil
1	shallot or green onion (include half the green tops), finely chopped
2 TEASPOONS	minced fresh ginger
12 OUNCES	langoustines (large prawns) or cooked bay shrimp
¾ CUP (6 OUNCES)	ricotta cheese
⅓ CUP	plain yogurt or fresh white goat cheese at room temperature
2 TABLESPOONS	minced fresh cilantro, plus fresh cilantro sprigs for garnish
1	avocado, peeled, pitted, and diced
1	mango, peeled, cut from the pit, and diced

PREPARE the crêpes. In a medium skillet over medium heat, heat the oil and sauté the shallot or green onion and ginger for 1 minute. Add the langoustines or bay shrimp and sauté for 2 minutes, or until just heated through.

In a medium bowl, mix together the ricotta, yogurt or goat cheese, and minced cilantro. Gently mix in the langoustine mixture, avocado, and mango. Spoon ½ cup of filling in a ribbon down the center of each crêpe and roll up. Garnish with cilantro leaves. Serve at room temperature or chilled.

Makes 8 crêpes; serves 4

SHRIMP & JICAMA CRÊPES

the delightful crunch of jicama enhances tender seafood crêpes, which make a spectacular brunch or lunch entrée partnered by an avocado, pink grapefruit, and papaya salad.

EIGHT 6- OR 7-INCH	savory crêpes (see page 13)
1 TABLESPOON	extra-virgin olive oil
2	shallots or green onions, finely chopped
2 TEASPOONS	minced fresh ginger
½ CUP (4 OUNCES)	ricotta cheese
½ CUP (4 OUNCES)	fresh white goat cheese or light cream cheese at room temperature
½ CUP (2 OUNCES)	shredded Gruyère, Jarlsberg, or Emmenthal cheese
10 OUNCES	cooked bay shrimp
1	small jicama, peeled and finely chopped (about ¾ cup)
¼ CUP	minced fresh flat-leaf parsley, plus parsley sprigs for garnish
2 TEASPOONS	minced fresh dill, or ½ teaspoon dried dill

prepare the crêpes. Preheat the oven to 350 degrees F. In a small skillet over medium heat, heat the oil and sauté the shallots or green onions and ginger for 1 to 2 minutes, or until soft. In a medium bowl, combine the cheeses, shrimp, jicama, parsley, dill, and shallot mixture.

Spoon ½ cup of the filling in a ribbon down the center of each crêpe and roll up. Arrange in a greased 9-by-13-inch baking dish. Bake in the oven for 10 to 15 minutes, or until heated through. Garnish with parsley sprigs and serve at once.

Makes 8 crêpes; serves 4

83

dessert crêpes

MANGO-PISTACHIO CRÊPES WITH SORBET 85

CARAMELIZED APPLE & CALVADOS CRÊPES 87

STRAWBERRY & BLUEBERRY CRÊPES WITH RASPBERRY SAUCE 88

HACIENDA CRÊPES SUZETTE 89

CHERRIES JUBILEE CRÊPES 91

PARISIAN STREET VENDOR CRÊPES 92

ORANGE CUSTARD CRÊPES 93

PEACH CRÊPES WITH ALMOND PRALINE 95

GRAND MARNIER SOUFFLÉ HALF-MOON CRÊPES 96

ICE CREAM CRÊPES WITH CARAMEL SAUCE 99

CHOCOLATE SOUFFLÉ HALF-MOON CRÊPES 101

CHOCOLATE & HAZELNUT PRALINE CRÊPES 103

ESPRESSO CRÊPES WITH CHOCOLATE COFFEE BEANS 104

LEMON CURD & KIWI FRUIT CRÊPES 106

MANGO-PISTACHIO CRÊPES WITH SORBET

in South Africa, where the mangoes are sublime, I was served an unusual dessert at the elite French restaurant Chez Patrice in the city of Santown: hot, sliced mangoes gilded with a honey-caramel sauce, crunchy with roasted pistachios, and accompanied with sorbet. The idea adapts admirably to crêpes.

SIX 6- OR 7-INCH	dessert crêpes (see page 16)
⅓ CUP	sugar
¼ CUP	pistachios, shelled
3 TABLESPOONS	honey
¼ CUP	water
1	large mango, peeled, cut from the pit, and sliced
	Lemon, orange, or mango sorbet, or vanilla bean ice cream (optional)

prepare the crêpes. Cover them with aluminum foil and keep warm in a 200-degree-F oven, or cover and reheat them in a baking pan in a preheated 325-degree-F oven for 5 to 10 minutes, or until heated through.

In a large, heavy skillet, heat the sugar over medium heat until it melts and turns amber. Add the nuts, shake to toast them for 1 minute, then gently pour in the honey and water, shaking the pan and heating over low heat until blended. Add the mango slices and cook until heated through.

Place 1 crêpe on each of 6 warm dessert plates. Place a spoonful of mangoes in the center of each and fold 2 sides over. Top with a spoonful of sauce with nuts. Place a scoop of sorbet or ice cream alongside, if desired. Serve at once.

Makes 6 crêpes; serves 6

CARAMELIZED APPLE & CALVADOS CRÊPES

better than warm apple pie, these caramelized apple crêpes are scented with apple brandy.

EIGHT 6- OR 7-INCH	dessert crêpes, flavored with Calvados (see page 16)
3	Granny Smith or Golden Delicious apples
2 TABLESPOONS	unsalted butter
⅓ CUP	granulated sugar
1 TABLESPOON	Calvados or Cognac (optional)
½ TEASPOON	ground cinnamon (optional)
3 TABLESPOONS	hazelnuts, toasted, skinned, and chopped (see page 46)
	Powdered sugar for dusting
	Whipped cream or vanilla ice cream for garnish

prepare the crêpes. Cover them with aluminum foil and keep warm in a 200-degree-F oven, or cover and reheat them in a baking pan in a preheated 325-degree-F oven for 5 to 10 minutes, or until heated through.

Peel, core, and slice the apples. In a large skillet, melt the butter over medium heat until it starts to sizzle. Add the apples, sprinkle with the sugar, and cook until the sugar turns amber, about 3 minutes. Gently sauté the apples and sugar until tender, another 4 to 5 minutes. Gently mix in the optional Calvados or Cognac and cinnamon, if you like; add the nuts. Set aside.

Arrange a few slices of caramelized apples on one-quarter of each crêpe. Fold each crêpe in half twice so it is triangular in shape. Sprinkle with powdered sugar. Top with a dollop of whipped cream or ice cream and serve at once.

Makes 8 crêpes; serves 4

STRAWBERRY & BLUEBERRY CRÊPES WITH RASPBERRY SAUCE

berry- and ice cream–filled crêpes on a pool of raspberry sauce are a delectable sweet for any time of day: brunch, lunch, or dinner. If the sauce is made in advance, these crêpes assemble swiftly.

EIGHT 6- OR 7-INCH   dessert crêpes (see page 16)

RASPBERRY SAUCE

1½ CUPS   fresh raspberries or thawed unsweetened frozen raspberries

Sugar

1 TEASPOON   framboise, if desired

2 CUPS   mixed fresh blueberries and sliced strawberries

Sugar

1 PINT   vanilla ice cream or vanilla-and-raspberry frozen yogurt

prepare the crêpes. *To PREPARE THE SAUCE:* Place the berries in a blender or food processor and purée. Push the purée through a sieve; discard the seeds. Sweeten to taste with 1 to 2 teaspoons sugar and stir in the framboise, if using.

Spoon a pool of sauce on each of 4 dessert plates. In a medium bowl, toss the berries with sugar to taste. Place a crêpe on a plate. Place a spoonful each of ice cream and berries in the center of the crêpe and fold over 2 sides. Repeat with the remaining crêpes. Place 2 filled crêpes on each plate and serve at once.

Makes 8 crêpes; serves 4

HACIENDA CRÊPES SUZETTE

when I dined with friends at the elegant Hacienda de Morales in Mexico City years ago, the chef flamed these citrus-imbued crêpes at tableside. I could hardly wait to reproduce them in my home.

TWELVE 6- OR 7-INCH	dessert crêpes (see page 16)
¼ CUP	sugar
1	orange zest strip
1	lime zest strip
2 TABLESPOONS	butter
2 TABLESPOONS	fresh lime juice
1 CUP	fresh orange juice
2 TABLESPOONS	Cointreau
2 TABLESPOONS	Cognac
2 TABLESPOONS	Grand Marnier

prepare the crêpes. In a large skillet or a chafing dish over medium heat, heat the sugar with the orange and lime strips until the sugar melts and turns amber. Add the butter, lime juice, and orange juice, and cook, stirring until blended and slightly reduced. Fold the crêpes into quarters and arrange them in an overlapping circle in the pan.

In a small pan, combine the liqueurs, warm over low heat, ignite with a match, and spoon the flaming liquid over the crêpes. Serve 3 crêpes on each of 4 warm dessert plates and spoon the sauce over. Serve at once.

Makes 12 crêpes; serves 4

CHERRIES JUBILEE CRÊPES

during their fleeting season, sweet cherries lend a luxurious fruitiness to crêpes.

EIGHT 6- OR 7-INCH	dessert crêpes, flavored with brandy or kirsch if desired (see page 16)
3 TABLESPOONS	unsalted butter
3 TABLESPOONS	sugar
½ CUP	water
¼ CUP	ruby Port
12 OUNCES (1½ CUPS)	Bing cherries, pitted
1 TABLESPOON	fresh lemon juice
3 TABLESPOONS	brandy or Cognac
	Vanilla frozen yogurt or ice cream

prepare the crêpes. In a large skillet over medium heat, melt the butter until it foams. Sprinkle in the sugar and cook for 1 to 2 minutes. Pour in the water and wine and cook until it reduces to the consistency of a syrup. Add the cherries, heat through, and stir in the lemon juice. Fold the crêpes into triangles and add them to the skillet, coating them in the sauce.

Push the crêpes to one side. Heat the brandy, ignite with a match, and spoon the flaming brandy over the sauce. When the flames subside, serve 2 crêpes and a spoonful or two of sauce on each plate. Top with a dollop of frozen yogurt or ice cream. Serve at once.

Makes 8 crêpes; serves 4

PARISIAN STREET VENDOR CRÊPES

throughout Paris and the French countryside, street vendors with carts turn out crêpes in a flash. A large round grill about 12 inches in diameter is used for cooking the crêpes. The baker pours on the batter and swiftly spreads it with a flat paddle. Each crêpe is cooked, filled, and served in minutes. To serve the same kind of crêpes for brunch or dessert, set out warm crêpes with assorted toppings for guests to fill their own.

SIXTEEN 6- OR 7-INCH   Dessert crêpes (see page 16)

FILLINGS
Apricot or strawberry jam
Powdered sugar and fresh lemon juice
Cointreau, rum, or brandy
Fresh strawberries, blueberries, or raspberries

TOPPINGS
Whipped cream, vanilla ice cream, or frozen vanilla yogurt
Shredded bittersweet chocolate
Toasted sliced almonds, chopped hazelnuts, or
Almond Praline (see page 95)

prepare the crêpes. Cover them with aluminum foil and keep warm in a 200-degree-F oven, or cover and reheat them in a baking pan in a preheated 325-degree-F oven for 5 to 10 minutes, or until heated through.

Set out the fillings and toppings and let guests create their own desserts.

Makes 16 crêpes; serves 8

ORANGE CUSTARD CRÊPES

a luscious orange custard cream fills crêpes for a taste-tingling midwinter dessert.

EIGHT 6- OR 7-INCH   dessert crêpes (see page 16)

ORANGE CUSTARD

2	egg yolks, lightly beaten
¼ CUP	sugar
⅓ CUP	fresh orange juice
3 TABLESPOONS	orange juice concentrate, thawed
1 TABLESPOON	fresh lemon juice
2 TEASPOONS	grated orange zest
1 TABLESPOON	butter
¾ CUP	heavy (whipping) cream

GARNISH
Blood orange, mandarin, or tangerine segments
Pistachios or toasted slivered almonds

prepare the crêpes.

TO MAKE THE ORANGE CUSTARD: In a double boiler, whisk together the egg yolks, sugar, orange juice, orange juice concentrate, lemon juice, orange zest, and butter. Cook over barely simmering water, stirring, until thickened. Refrigerate until cold.

In a deep bowl, whip the cream until it forms soft peaks. Fold in the orange custard and whisk until soft peaks form again. Spoon one-eighth of the custard in a ribbon down the center of each crêpe and roll up. Garnish with citrus segments and nuts.

Makes 8 crêpes; serves 4

PEACH CRÊPES WITH ALMOND PRALINE

the crunch of praline contrasts with juicy peaches and whipped cream cheese for a winning summertime dessert.

EIGHT 6- OR 7-INCH   dessert crêpes (see page 16)

ALMOND PRALINE
⅓ CUP   granulated sugar
⅓ CUP   chopped almonds

⅓ CUP (3 OUNCES)   light cream cheese at room temperature
2 TABLESPOONS   powdered sugar
1 TABLESPOON   amaretto or brandy, or ¼ teaspoon almond extract
¾ CUP   heavy (whipping) cream
3   peaches or nectarines, peeled, pitted, and diced

prepare the crêpes.

To make the almond praline: In a small, heavy skillet over medium heat, heat the sugar until it melts. Add the nuts, shake to coat, and cook until the syrup turns a light amber color. Immediately pour onto a sheet of buttered aluminum foil; let cool. Chop finely or pulverize in a blender or food processor.

In a small, deep bowl, cream the cheese until fluffy. Beat in the sugar and amaretto, brandy, or almond extract. Pour in the cream and beat until stiff peaks form. Fold in two-thirds of the peaches. Reserve 2 tablespoons of the praline and fold in the remainder.

Spoon one-eighth of the peaches and cream on each crêpe and roll up. Spoon some of the remaining peaches alongside, and sprinkle with the reserved praline.

Makes 8 crêpes; serves 4

GRAND MARNIER SOUFFLÉ
HALF-MOON CRÊPES

a fast-to-assemble orange soufflé billows inside sweet crêpes for an impressive company dessert. Adorn the plate with strawberries, raspberries, or a bright nasturtium blossom or sprig of lavender from the garden. Among friends, you might enjoy serving the crêpes on one plate at the center of the table and letting everyone help themselves.

EIGHT 6- OR 7-INCH	dessert crêpes (see page 16)

GRAND MARNIER SOUFFLÉ

3	eggs, separated
⅛ TEASPOON	salt
⅛ TEASPOON	cream of tartar
3 TABLESPOONS	sugar
⅓ CUP	orange juice concentrate, thawed
2 TABLESPOONS	Grand Marnier

GARNISH
Powdered sugar
Fresh strawberries or raspberries (optional)
Whipped cream or ice cream (optional)

prepare the crêpes.
TO MAKE THE SOUFFLÉ: Preheat the oven to 350 degrees F. In a large bowl, beat the egg whites until foamy. Add the salt and cream of tartar and beat until soft peaks form. Add 2 tablespoons of the sugar and beat until stiff, glossy peaks form. In a medium bowl, beat the egg yolks until pale and beat in the remaining 1 tablespoon sugar. Stir in the orange concentrate and Grand Marnier. Mix one-third of the egg whites into the yolks; gently fold in the remaining whites.

Place the crêpes on a lightly buttered baking sheet. Spoon 2 rounded spoonfuls of soufflé on one half of each crêpe and fold the other half over gently to cover.

Bake in the oven for **10** minutes, or until puffed and set. Dust with powdered sugar. Garnish with berries and top with whipped cream or vanilla ice cream, if desired. Serve at once.

Makes 8 crêpes; serves 4

ICE CREAM CRÊPES WITH CARAMEL SAUCE

caramel sauce tops these ice cream–filled crêpes showered with toasted pecans. Keep the various components on hand for a spur-of-the moment dessert.

SIX 6- OR 7-INCH	dessert crêpes (see page 16)
	CARAMEL SAUCE
½ CUP	sugar
⅓ CUP	half-and-half
2 TABLESPOONS	unsalted butter
1 TABLESPOON	light corn syrup
1 PINT	coffee or vanilla bean ice cream or frozen yogurt
3 TABLESPOONS	pecans or walnuts, toasted (see Note), or Almond Praline (see page 95)

prepare the crêpes.

TO MAKE THE CARAMEL SAUCE: In a small, heavy saucepan over medium heat, heat the sugar until it melts and turns a light amber color. Carefully stir in the half-and-half, butter, and corn syrup. Cook and stir until smooth and slightly thickened, about 2 minutes.

Place each crêpe on a dessert plate. Place 2 spoonfuls of the ice cream on each crêpe and fold gently to cover. Drizzle the caramel sauce over the crêpes and sprinkle with nuts. Serve at once.

Makes 6 crêpes; serves 6

NOTE: To toast pecans and walnuts, place the nuts in a baking dish and bake in a preheated 325-degree-F oven for 8 to 10 minutes, or until golden.

CHOCOLATE SOUFFLÉ
HALF-MOON CRÊPES

pillows of warm chocolate soufflé folded inside dark chocolate pancakes make an ethereal dessert. Top with a pouf of whipped cream or a scoop of ice cream. These crêpes may be assembled 1 hour in advance. For an extra flourish, sprinkle them with a few fresh raspberries.

TWELVE 6- OR 7-INCH chocolate crêpes (see page 16)

CHOCOLATE SOUFFLÉ

4 OUNCES	bittersweet chocolate, finely chopped
4	eggs, separated
⅛ TEASPOON	salt
⅛ TEASPOON	cream of tartar
5 TABLESPOONS	sugar
1 TEASPOON	vanilla extract

GARNISH
Powdered sugar for dusting
Whipped cream or vanilla or coffee ice cream

101

prepare the crêpes.

To make the chocolate soufflé: In a double boiler over barely simmering water, melt the chocolate. Let cool to room temperature. In a large bowl, beat the egg whites until foamy. Add the salt and cream of tartar and beat until soft peaks form. Add 3 tablespoons of the sugar and beat until stiff, glossy peaks form. In a medium bowl, beat the egg yolks until pale. Beat in the remaining 2 tablespoons sugar. Stir in the chocolate and vanilla. Mix one-third of the egg whites into the yolks, then gently fold in the remaining whites.

Place the crêpes on 2 lightly buttered baking sheets. Spoon 2 rounded spoonfuls of soufflé on one half of each crêpe and fold the other half over gently to cover. If desired, assemble to this point and let sit at room temperature for 1 hour before baking.

To bake, preheat the oven to 350 degrees F. Bake in the oven for 10 minutes, or until puffed and set. Dust with powdered sugar. Serve at once, topped with whipped cream or vanilla ice cream.

Makes 12 crêpes; serves 6

CHOCOLATE & HAZELNUT PRALINE CRÊPES

chocolate melting over caramelized hazelnuts is a sumptuous filling for warm, sweet crêpes. A cool topping of vanilla bean ice cream or rum-scented whipped cream lends a nice contrast.

EIGHT 6- OR 7-INCH	chocolate crêpes (see page 16)
2 TEASPOONS	butter
2 TABLESPOONS	sugar
½ CUP (2½ OUNCES)	hazelnuts, toasted, skinned, and chopped (see page 46), or almonds, chopped
4 OUNCES	bittersweet chocolate, grated
	Whipped cream flavored with rum or brandy, vanilla bean ice cream, or coffee frozen yogurt

prepare the crêpes. Preheat the oven to 375 degrees F. In a small skillet over medium heat, melt the butter with the sugar. Add the nuts and sauté until they are golden brown and the syrup turns amber. Let cool and chop finely with a large chef's knife.

Mix the caramelized nuts and chocolate together in a medium bowl and spoon about 2 tablespoons of the mixture into the center of each crêpe. Fold crêpes like an envelope and place in a buttered 9-by-13-inch baking dish. Bake in the oven for 6 to 8 minutes, or until heated through. Serve at once with a topping of flavored whipped cream, ice cream, or frozen yogurt.

Makes 8 crêpes; serves 4

ESPRESSO CRÊPES WITH CHOCOLATE COFFEE BEANS

create your own chocolate-coated coffee beans to garnish this quick-to-assemble dessert, or buy them from a specialty foods store. With the crêpes, candy, and chocolate sauce on hand, it takes only minutes to prepare this dessert.

SIX 9- OR 10-INCH	dessert crêpes, flavored with brandy or rum if desired (see page 16)

CHOCOLATE-COATED COFFEE BEANS

½ OUNCe	bittersweet chocolate, chopped
¼ TEASPOON	unsalted butter
2 TABLESPOONS	coffee beans

CHOCOLATE SAUCE

4 OUNCES	bittersweet chocolate, chopped
3 TABLESPOONS	strong brewed coffee
3 TABLESPOONS	half-and-half
2 TABLESPOONS	light corn syrup

1 PINT	coffee or chocolate frozen yogurt
	Whipped cream for garnish (optional)

prepare the crêpes. Cover them with aluminum foil and keep warm in a 200-degree-F oven, or cover and reheat them in a baking pan in a preheated 325-degree-F oven for 5 to 10 minutes, or until heated through.

To make the chocolate beans: Melt the chocolate and butter in a double boiler over barely simmering water. With a fork slipped under each bean, dip the bean into the chocolate to coat and place on buttered aluminum foil to cool. Repeat with the remaining beans until all are coated. Refrigerate until set, about 15 minutes.

To MAKE THE CHOCOLATE SAUCE: Combine the chocolate, coffee, half-and-half, and corn syrup in a double boiler and heat over barely simmering water until the chocolate is melted; stir to blend.

For each serving, place 1 crêpe on a plate, fold in half, then fold again, forming a fan shape. Place a scoop of ice cream and a dollop of whipped cream in the center, if desired. Drizzle chocolate sauce in a wavy pattern across the crêpe. Garnish with 2 or 3 chocolate coffee beans. Repeat with the remaining crêpes. Serve at once.

Makes 6 crêpes; serves 6

Lemon Curd & Kiwi Fruit Crêpes

lemon-flavored crêpes envelop a traditional English tart filling in this delicious dessert, which would also be fun to serve for afternoon tea.

EIGHT 6- OR 7-INCH	dessert crêpes, flavored with lemon zest (see page 16)
	LEMON CURD
3	eggs
3	egg yolks
½ CUP	sugar
2 TEASPOONS	grated lemon zest
¾ CUP	fresh lemon juice
½ CUP (1 STICK)	butter, at room temperature, cut into tablespoon-sized pieces
2	kiwi fruit, peeled and sliced

prepare the crêpes.

TO MAKE THE LEMON CURD: In a medium bowl, beat the eggs, egg yolks, sugar, lemon zest, and lemon juice together. Place the bowl over a pan of barely simmering water and whisk until the mixture thickens, about 10 minutes. Remove from the heat and whisk in the butter, 1 piece at a time.

Spoon ¼ cup of lemon curd in a ribbon down the center of each crêpe and roll up. Top with kiwi fruit slices.

Makes 8 crêpes; serves 4

table of equivalents

The exact equivalents in the following tables have been rounded for convenience.

LIQUID AND DRY MEASURES

U.S.	METRIC
¼ TEASPOON	1.25 MILLILITERS
½ TEASPOON	2.5 MILLILITERS
1 TEASPOON	5 MILLILITERS
1 TABLESPOON (3 TSP.)	15 MILLILITERS
1 FLUID OUNCE (2 TSP.)	30 MILLILITERS
¼ CUP	60 MILLILITERS
⅓ CUP	80 MILLILITERS
1 CUP	240 MILLILITERS
1 PINT (2 CUPS)	480 MILLILITERS
1 QUART (4 CUPS, 32 OZ.)	960 MILLILITERS
1 GALLON (4 QUARTS)	3.84 LITERS
1 OUNCE (BY WEIGHT)	28 GRAMS
¼ POUND (4 OZ.)	114 GRAMS
1 POUND	454 GRAMS
2.2 POUNDS	1 KILOGRAM

OVEN TEMPERATURES

FAHRENHEIT	CELSIUS	GAS
250	120	½
275	140	1
300	150	2
325	160	3
350	180	4
375	190	5
400	200	6
425	220	7
450	230	8
475	240	9
500	260	10

LENGTH MEASURES

U.S.	METRIC
⅛ INCH	3 MILLIMETERS
¼ INCH	6 MILLIMETERS
½ INCH	12 MILLIMETERS
1 INCH	2.5 CENTIMETERS

index